THE MUSIC OF THE LAWS

DANIEL KORNSTEIN

*The Music of
the Laws*

FOREWORD BY
HON. ROBERT H. BORK

NEW YORK EVEREST HOUSE PUBLISHERS

Many of the essays in this book originally appeared in slightly altered form in The New York Law Journal.

Published by Everest House, New York
Published simultaneously in Canada by
Beaverbooks, Don Mills, Ontario
Manufactured in the United States of America
Designed by Abe Lerner
First Edition   FG 1082

Library of Congress Cataloging in Publication Data:

Kornstein, Daniel.
The music of the laws.

1. Law—United States—Methodology—Ad-
dresses, essays, lectures.   2. Law—United
States—Interpretation and construction—Ad-
dresses, essays, lectures.   I. Title.
KF380.K67   1982   349.73'01'8   82-11904
ISBN 0-89696-185-0   347.30018

FOR

SUSAN

MY LIFE PARTNER

CONTENTS

FOREWORD

By Hon. Robert H. Bork, United States Circuit Judge

THE essays in this book range entertainingly over a wide range of subjects in or related to law, yet the effect is not diffuseness but rather a sense of seeing the facets of a single topic. That is because the pieces are bound together by two unifying themes. One is the play upon the topics selected of a lively, informed, and consistent mind. Daniel Kornstein clearly loves the law; indeed, he is infatuated with it, with its diversity, with its competing ideas, with the personalities who make and mar it. A single voice talking about any variety of subjects which happen to fascinate the speaker will impose a unity on those subjects, the unity of that man's mind and temper. But there is a different kind of unity here, too, for despite apparent diversity—the discussion ranges over the interplay of different concepts of liberty in constitutional law, Ayn Rand's view of law, military justice, confusion in the First Amendment, and much more—in various ways and from different angles Mr. Kornstein keeps returning to the teasing, at times agitating, paradox of courts with the power to set at naught the policies and actions of the people's representatives.

Despite the labors of judges and scholars, labors which proceed unremittingly and produce a cascade of literature

9

nobody has quite put us at ease with the institution of judicial review. Perhaps no one can. On the other hand, few of us are at ease with the idea of abandoning judicial review. Americans grow angry with their courts but very few would be willing to take from them completely the power first asserted in 1803, sparingly used for decades, and now freely exercised. With us, the idea of a Constitution is almost, not quite but almost, synonymous with the idea of a Supreme Court applying it as law against some manifestations of democratic will. Yet we remain uneasy and, at times, bitter and restive under judicial authority. This has been true throughout our history, from the assaults of the Jeffersonians on the Federalist courts of their time to the most recent proposals to remove jurisdiction in areas where the federal courts are thought by many to have exceeded any mandate arguably given by the Constitution. Americans fear majority tyranny but they also resent being told, without adequate explanation, that there are major aspects of their lives, their moral environment, the values that are to reign in their communities, which they may not determine for themselves. As much as they revere the Constitution, large segments of the American public have come to believe that courts have imposed values and rules that do not have their roots in the Constitution, that cannot be justified, much less said to be compelled, by any fair interpretation of that document. Whether this is or is not the case, it is important when large numbers of people come to believe that it is and when they find articulate spokesmen and strong political representation.

It is interesting that the main intellectual defense offered for the judicial behavior under criticism does not deny the main charge—that the rules being laid down do not come from the Constitution. Instead, the academic writers offer something like a defense of confession and avoidance. Various major constitutional commentators have published theories, and one may be certain that more are on the way, designed to demonstrate that courts should not be limited to deriving the meaning of the written, historical Constitution but should be creating and expanding individual rights from sources such as natural law or conventional morality or the nature of a truly democratic process or something else. This non-interpretivist view of the judicial function has not, in my judgment, been satisfactorily worked out as yet (one of the problems being that each non-interpretivist professor keeps punching holes in the theories of all other non-interpretivist professors), but then neither, so far as I know, has any interpretivist theory been brought to a full and satisfactory statement.

It is too soon to say what the outcome of current political battles about the courts is likely to be, but surely it is both beneficial and exciting that the judicial role has come under powerful intellectual scrutiny and that there is at least a possibility that some version of an interpretivist or non-interpretivist theory may establish intellectual hegemony. If so, that development would in time heavily affect both the courts' performance and the political response to it. While I have never been persuaded that ideas are omnipotent in the world, unless the word "idea" is broadened to include so much that it becomes merely another term for "human reaction," their power must not be underestimated, and that is particularly so in a field like law.

In this book you will find ideas, a great many ideas. And, widely though he roams, Mr. Kornstein's paths usually lead back in some way to the problem of the appropriate role of the judge, the proper boundaries of judicial supremacy. Whether the subject is Sir Isaiah Berlin's relevance to American constitutional law or the judicial careers of Holmes, Frankfurter, and Douglas, the reader is provoked to think about what a judge's duty is, what we want our judges to be. It is important that books like this be written and read because the work of courts and the virtues appropriate to them are too little understood. Courts, as well as legislatures and executives, are capable of behaving badly, indeed of performing unconstitutionally, but, unlike the other branches, courts are subject to no external check—other than criticism. It is important that public understanding be informed and criticism accurately directed. This book helps.

This is not to say that the reader will necessarily agree with all of Mr. Kornstein's views. I found myself in silent debate on almost every page. But that is one of the merits of this book: it provokes thought, agreement, and dissent. Mr. Kornstein has chosen the figure of music to express a way of looking at the law. Since he is an old friend and a former student of mine, it is a pleasure to find that he dances the patterns so well.

Kepler's Spirit

At the start of the seventeenth century, astronomer Johannes Kepler watched the skies and heard the "music of the spheres." Kepler, intellectual heir of the magnificent Copernicus and the industrious Tycho Brahe, worked in Tycho's observatory on a little Danish island where he discovered basic laws of planetary motion. Equipped with penetrating vision where others had seen nothing, Kepler unified disparate phenomena, laid bare age-old secrets, and compelled nature to order. Kepler sought and claimed to find mathematical harmonies between the orbits of the planets. For Kepler, as for the Pythagoreans almost 2,000 years earlier, the planets filled the air with celestial music, each planet singing its own tune. Perhaps the spirit that so moved Kepler can animate and deepen inquiry in any field, including law.

Just as Kepler heard the "music of the spheres," so too may we be able to hear the "music of the laws." To be sure, law often seems chaotic and confused, an incomprehensible and incoherent welter of apparently contradictory and ever-changing rules, traditions, and practices. The confusion is heightened by the increasing number and complexity of laws reaching into every corner of our lives and made necessary by improving technology and changed social policies. And yet, despite this apparent cacophony of laws, there may well be mysterious harmonies, rhythms, and relationships to be discerned. The quest for such harmonies—the search for order out of chaos—may allow us to approach law from a different perspective and with new sensitivity. But to hear the "music of the laws"—to see the interconnectedness of apparently unrelated legal phenomena—we need something of Kepler's spirit.

Kepler's spirit is marked by several noteworthy qualities. He sought understanding: he wanted to grasp the structure of the universe. He was bold: he had the audacity to conceive of law and order amid a jumble of phenomena. He then had the creative genius to uncover some of the underlying patterns. At times coldly rational, Kepler had a fertile imagination that triggered the conception of new theoretical systems. But Kepler also knew that theories must fit facts: he sacrificed even his most beloved mathematical hypotheses when he saw that they did not fit observational data. These are some of the spiritual parts needed to manufacture Keplerian hearing aids for listening to the "music of the laws."

We should try to understand the law. We need a strong will to understand the structure of the legal universe. This need to understand should impel us to look at the law and ask, with a child's simplicity, "Why?" Answers should be forthcoming. Of course there may be deep mysteries and profound paradoxes in the law. But for the most part we are entitled to reasonable explanations. Where existing explanations are unsatisfactory, we should seek better explanations. Nothing less will do for the inquiring mind's search for understanding.

Like Kepler, we need to be bold enough to envision the possibility that there is law and order in the legal universe.

We cannot be deterred by the bewildering array of legal doctrines. We need a passion for generalization and a horror of anarchy, without overgeneralizing at the expense of true diversity. We must have a will to give reasons for what appears irrational, to find order in chaos, and unity in variety without denying that variety. Of course, we must be wary of turning Kepler's spirit into an unhealthy legal monism. Kepler's spirit should not be understood as an ironclad rule that all phenomena in law or elsewhere must be explained by a fundamental principle. The world is too varied and human beings have too many competing values to conclude that one principle or belief can explain all. But that is no argument against looking for underlying patterns.

To find the underlying patterns in law, we need Kepler's attitude of creative simplicity. Kepler had a childlike readiness to see things anew, to look at problems with fresh eyes. His ability to find new relations between familiar things and to combine what he learned in unlikely ways made him more apt to hit upon truly startling ideas. Approaching law in Kepler's spirit, we may start to see meanings that have eluded us up to now. We may perceive genuine connections between things as superficially disparate as law and literature, mathematics, philosophy, or even music. We may be able to grasp legal developments in terms of religious trends in society. By relaxing our normally rigid mental compartments, we may find a close and unexpected nexus between, say, constitutional law and an essay on political theory, or the litigation process and humor, or a judge's performance on the bench and his inner mental life. This is not to say that law and the universe form a seamless web, but it does suggest that there may be more connections between law and other fields than we have yet fully appreciated.

Once new legal patterns and relations are perceived, it may be possible to dream of harmonies that would unravel the mysterious complexities of the legal universe. Insights drawn from an essay on political theory—for instance, Isaiah Berlin's "Two Concepts of Liberty"—may unlock and illuminate all of constitutional law. Interpretive methods in literary criticism or musical performance may yield a glimpse of an overall theory of interpretation of which legal interpretation is only a constituent part. The attitudes and preconditions for originality and creativity in other fields tell us what circumstances are conducive to creativity in law. If and when such new and mysterious harmonies are discovered, we are entitled, like Kepler, to be ecstatic.

But the ecstasy over theory must be tempered by the facts. Kepler was one of the first Renaissance thinkers to insist that theory fit facts. He was a visionary disciplined by appeal to experience, an empiricist motivated by deep vision. With his stress on observation and empirical data, Kepler departed radically from the ancient Greeks and medievalists, who had believed that the mind, not experience, was the source of basic principles. We see the ghost of Kepler's spirit in the most famous modern example of fundamental legal theory adapting itself to the facts: the Supreme Court's celebrated 1954 school desegregation decision in *Brown* v. *Board of Education*. In that case the Court overruled the old "separate but equal" doctrine on the ground that psychological and sociological evidence showed that the factual premise of the old rule was false, that in fact, "Separate educational facilities are inherently unequal." The process of reexamining factual premises and adapting law to actual facts applies to all areas of law. Every branch of law—contracts, torts, antitrust, domestic relations, criminal law, and so forth—depends on many factual assumptions that, if wrong, could change the outcome of legal decisions. If legal theory does not fit the facts, then it is the legal theory and not the facts that should yield.

But we have to be careful about what we mean by "facts." A powerful intellectual construct, like a legal or scientific theory, should not be lightly abandoned if a fact or experiment that contradicts the theory is reported. The reason is that an isolated fact inconsistent with a large body of knowledge stands a good chance of being wrong. Particularly when appellate courts frame new rules of law based on "facts" found by lower courts, lawyers need to be what Jerome Frank called "fact-skeptics."

Due to the constant reexamination of theory and fact, every field of law is incomplete. In this sense, the conclusions reached in law, when looked at closely, are provisional and tentative only. Next week's decision or law review article can turn a whole field upside down, shaking out any number of immutable ideas and installing new bodies of dogma. This flux is at least one reason why law is neither dull nor boring. It is this continual excitement that makes law engrossing, that keeps bright people at it, and that ought to be at the center of law practice.

As an example of modern scientific inquiry, Kepler's spirit may heighten our awareness of the differences between objective and subjective legal thinking. Scientific discovery tends to separate facts and values, and move us closer to positivism. If the orbits of the planets were beautiful to Kepler, to later scientists those orbits were simply facts, neither beautiful nor ugly. Although law and legal judgments are intertwined with values, there have always been powerful efforts to minimize the subjective elements of law. A hundred years ago, for instance, Holmes argued for an entirely objective theory of law, one that paid little or no attention to the subjective intent of the individuals involved. Today's legal objectivists pay lip service to

Holmes's goals, but, oddly enough and apparently without realizing it, describe as objective what Holmes viewed as subjective, for example, legislative intent. The answer may involve finding reliable standards for subjective judgment; subjective need not mean the same thing as arbitrary. Perhaps caprice in the law can be taught to bend before a kind of educated subjectivism.

On another level, the richness of Kepler's imagery—the musical metaphor—enabled men to think differently and more fruitfully about old concepts, in the hope of gaining more understanding. Kepler's musical metaphor is particularly suggestive for law. The word "music," like "law," conjures up a refined, elite endeavor, a product of man's intelligence at its most highly civilized and highly disciplined. Both music and law are sometimes seen as expressions of the sublime, the beautiful, and the eternal, a body of material based on the norms of Western civilization and the quiet pursuit of reason. Indeed, music has widened the sphere of legal ideas and enriched law with new images.

It is easy, for example, to sense the quasi-symphonic nature of law. Law offers us certain basic themes with a multitude of variations. Justice, mercy, due process of law, equality before the law—these are a few of the recurring major themes that serve as leitmotifs in law. Variations on these legal leitmotifs arise from different factual contexts as well as changed moral and social values. But the point is that the major themes recur.

From this viewpoint, the growth of the law might be compared to a fugue. The fugue starts with a theme based on a particular rule of law as sung by a particular judge. While the theme is still being sung, a second judicial voice modifies the first legal rule and introduces a secondary theme—a countersubject—which provides contrasts to the subject. As modifications of the legal rule occur, each judicial voice enters in turn, singing the theme, often accompanied by the countersubject in some other voice. After all the judicial voices have joined in, there are no "rules," only a collection of precedents that can be cited for either side of almost any legal proposition. The legal fugue—the play of principle and counterprinciple, the dialectic of theme and countertheme—fits neatly into the common law process. It shows how a confusing chorus may still be singing a basic theme.

There are even similarities between the participants in the musical and legal processes. Lawmakers can be likened to musical composers: both write the texts that others must interpret. And judges and lawyers are the performers of legal music. They look at the texts, be they constitutions, statutes, or judicial precedents, and put on those texts their own interpretations. In performing their roles, judges and lawyers interpret the legal texts much as instrumentalists interpret musical scores. There is lively debate in both fields about the performer's duty to be faithful to the composer's original intent.

If we do not hear the "music of the laws," perhaps that is because we are accustomed to it from birth. Whether the harmonies heard by Kepler really existed is not that important for us and for the law. For our purposes, we can leave Kepler to his solitary ecstasy over fictitious celestial harmonies. What is important for us is Kepler's attitude and spirit. Applying such a spirit to law, we may, if asked whether we hear the "music of the laws," answer as Kepler's mentor Tycho Brahe does in Alfred Noyes's poem "Watchers of the Skies":

> *We are like men that hear*
> *Disjointed notes of some supernal choir.*

THE MUSIC OF THE LAWS

1

Two Concepts of Liberty in Constitutional Law

Of all branches of philosophy, none helps us understand basic concepts of law more than political philosophy, with its focus on the relationship between the individual and the State. One of the most insightful of living political philosophers is Sir Isaiah Berlin, an Oxford don who writes with style about the humanities, the history of ideas, literature and philosophy. Berlin roams widely, but with a deft touch, over the full range of human intellectual activity. Ideas are what Berlin deals in, usually through the medium of essays.

One particular Berlin essay—entitled "Two Concepts of Liberty" and published in 1958 (reprinted in *Four Essays on Liberty*)—illuminates in extraordinary ways certain of the most fundamental aspects of American constitutional law. In that essay, Berlin divides liberty into two types, "positive" liberty encompassing political rights and "negative" liberty referring to individual liberties. For the most part, American constitutional law has totally failed to recognize the distinction drawn by Berlin, and the result has been confusion.

Candid application of Berlin's dichotomy between positive and negative liberty can help clarify this confusion.

Berlin's theory can serve, in the first instance, as an organizing principle for fundamental rights and for exposing the hidden tensions between them. It provides an analytical tool, of immense though unrealized power and scope, for helping to decide cases, to reconcile precedents, and to discern issues properly. It adds to our understanding of the relationship between the First Amendment and the other basic rights. It provides, finally, a comprehensive generalizing synthesis that facilitates constitutional theory and points that theory in a new and fruitful direction.

I

In "Two Concepts of Liberty," Berlin explains his dichotomy between negative and positive liberty. The negative notion of liberty, according to Berlin, involves individual freedom. It is negative in the sense of warding off interference, of preserving an area for private life independent of social control. It embodies the desire not to be impinged upon, to be left to oneself, to prevent the encroachment of public authority. Its purpose is to reserve a free area for action over which neither the State nor any authority must be allowed to interfere with an individual's activity. The wider the area of non-interference the wider the freedom.

If negative liberty focuses on the area of control, positive liberty deals with its source. The positive sense of liberty, as Berlin uses the term, means political rights. It stems from the wish on the part of the individual to be his own master, to have his life and decisions depend on himself, not on external forces of any kind. In short, positive liberty embodies the desire to be governed by oneself. It involves participation in the process by which a person's life is to be controlled.

The "great contrast" between positive and negative liberty is the difference between the questions "Who governs me?" and "How far does government interfere with me?" This contrast provides a means for classifying basic liberties as either positive or negative.

But genuine tension exists between positive and negative liberty. There is no necessary connection, as Berlin points out, between individual liberty and democratic rule. A benign despot may allow wide individual liberty, and a popularly elected government may greatly restrict individual freedom.

The "cardinal issue," according to Berlin, is that those who believe in negative liberty want to curb authority as such, and those who believe in positive liberty want authority placed in their own hands. "These are not two different interpretations of a single concept, but two profoundly divergent and irreconcilable attitudes to the ends of life." When positive and negative liberty collide, when the conflict between them prevents us from having both, we have to make some hard choices.

The "necessity and agony of choice" are unavoidable: that is Berlin's central lesson. It is natural and understandable to try to harmonize apparently incompatible values, to search for one all-embracing system that eliminates the sacrifice of certain values to the realization of others. For there is something jarring and dissatisfying about concluding that mankind's ideals collide; it destroys the desired harmony of the universe.

But Berlin says the belief in harmonizing the diverse ends of man is a delusion, a "demonstrably false" and often dogmatic monism that can lead to dangerous Procrustean solutions. Instead Berlin believes the possibility of conflict is inescapable because the ends of man are many, and not all of them are in principle compatible with each other.

Pluralism and its consequent necessity of choosing between absolute claims are what Berlin concludes give freedom of choice its immense value as an end in itself.

II

To see, in the first instance, how Berlin's dichotomy between positive and negative liberty works as an organizing principle, and how it provides a useful overview of constitutional law, it is necessary only to apply it to basic American freedoms in our Constitution.

The body of the Constitution contains several provisions relating to liberties. Provisions for the election and qualifications of public officials all cover positive liberty. The Republican Form of Government Clause in Article IV, although it may be unenforceable in court as one of the few remaining non-justiciable political questions, protects a positive liberty in that it purports to guaranty a republican form of government. Ratification and amendment procedures setting forth the methods of enactment and change of the Constitution also clearly pertain to positive liberties.

Some negative freedoms, too, find their source in the body of the Constitution. Sections 9 and 10 of Article I put limits on congressional and state power, which amount to protections for individual liberties. Article III ensures trial by jury in certain circumstances and erects particular requirements in treason prosecutions, including a prohibition against certain punishments. These provisions protect individual rights. Paradoxically, perhaps, the Constitution contains provisions prohibiting interference with the slave trade until 1808, which from the point of view of slaveholders and traders, should be a negative liberty provision.

Unlike the body of the Constitution, the Bill of Rights (excluding the First Amendment) contains protections only for negative liberties. Amendments 2 through 8 concern themselves almost entirely with individual liberties and not at all with political rights. Most of them underline procedural safeguards in criminal prosecutions or protect a zone of individual privacy. To be sure, the jury trial guarantees in the Sixth and Seventh Amendments have an element of participatory democracy and therefore positive liberty, but the main thrust of the right to trial by jury is the negative liberty trait of protecting the rights of the individual.

Later constitutional amendments fall into various categories. Those protecting positive liberties include extensions of the right to vote on the basis of race, sex, age and wealth, the grant of representation to the District of Columbia, and new mechanics for elections such as the Electoral College and direct election of senators. Negative liberty is embodied in the Thirteenth Amendment's prohibition against slavery and involuntary servitude and in the proposed Equal Rights Amendment. Section 1 of the Fourteenth Amendment belongs in a special category because the Privileges or Immunities Clause, the Due Process Clause, and the Equal Protection Clause, there made applicable to the states, have been interpreted to cover both positive and negative liberties through a process of selective incorporation. The rest of the post-Bill of Rights amendments relate to constitutional housekeeping. Significantly, most recent amendments extend the franchise in one way or another.

III

Useful and straightforward as Berlin's theory is outside the First Amendment area, within the realm of First Amendment activity it takes on even greater utility as well as far more complexity. Unlike other constitutional provisions, the First Amendment does not fit snugly into either of the categories positive or negative liberty. On its face, the Amendment encompasses several distinct subjects: religion, speech, press, assembly, and petition. Implied in the Amendment, as it has been interpreted, are additional liberties relating to freedom of thought and conscience, the right to express ideas and to be exposed to the ideas of others, and the right to associate with others for the expression of opinion.

The First Amendment's protection for so many different liberties makes generalization difficult but not impossible. Clause-by-clause analysis in terms of positive and negative liberty does yield results. It sheds light on the Framers' intent by a process of divining what they meant by looking at what they did. At the risk of overgeneralization, it can tentatively be suggested that the central thrust of the freedoms in the First Amendment, apart from the Religion Clauses, are positive in nature, and that interpretation of the Speech and Press Clauses should take that finding into account. At the same time, resolution of individual cases will involve choice between conflicting values of the highest order. Many of the problems in the First Amendment field can be explained in terms of difficult choices between positive and negative liberty.

Conventional First Amendment theory regarding speech and press appears at times to be woefully confused from the perspective of Berlin's theory. No coherent doctrine has emerged over the years. Instead we have a legacy of ad hoc decisions that often seems quite inconsistent in both results and rationales. In one case, Justice Brennan wrote for a majority that, "the protection given speech and press was fashioned to assure unfettered interchange of ideas for the bringing about of political and social changes desired by the people." Ten years later, the same Justice, without acknowledging any break with the past, wrote a Court opinion saying, "the guarantees for speech and press are not the preserve of political expression or comment upon public affairs, essential as those are to healthy government." At least on the surface, these statements seem irreconcilable in terms of the dichotomy between positive and negative liberty.

Equally irreconcilable in terms of Berlin's theory are holdings of what specific types of speech are protected by the First Amendment. For instance, obscenity and purely commercial speech are outside the political process as we usually understand that process, and therefore would appear to be within the scope of what we have described as negative liberty. Yet one is protected and one is not. How is it possible, in terms of positive and negative liberty, to square holding commercial speech covered by the First Amendment with excluding First Amendment protection for obscenity? Decisions like these make First Amendment doctrine look as if it lacks a central, unifying theory, as if it is a policy at war with itself.

The positive sense of liberty is the unacknowledged animating force behind what has come to be known as the Meiklejohn theory of the First Amendment. According to the late Professor Alexander Meiklejohn:

"The First Amendment does not protect a 'freedom to speak.' It protects the freedom of those activities of thought and communication by which we govern. It is concerned, not with a private right, but with a public power, a governmental responsibility."

From this point of view, first articulated by Meiklejohn in 1948, free speech is not protected for some intrinsic value of speech or individual liberty, but because it is a necessary condition for making informed decisions about matters of government, decisions that all citizens in a democracy are called on to make. Speech provides information, the raw material from which citizens can make self-governing choices. It is no exaggeration to regard the Meiklejohn theory as an interpretation of the First Amendment along positive liberty lines that are pure and classic.

Drawing on Meiklejohn's theory, the Supreme Court has, since its 1964 decision in *New York Times Co.* v. *Sullivan,* stressed the integral role of free speech in a democratic political system and the need for access to ideas and experience that citizens require for "[s]elf-governance." But even before Meiklejohn published *Free Speech and Its Relation to Self-Government,* the Court on occasion referred to similar functions of free speech and press. Scattered throughout the *United States Reports* are descriptions of free speech and press in terms of positive liberty.

In general, those cases excluding certain types of speech from First Amendment protection rest on the positive sense of liberty. In a group of 1973 cases, the Supreme Court expressly rejected the negative liberty argument "that government cannot legitimately impede an individual's desire to see or acquire obscene plays, movies and books," and once again chose the positive liberty interpretation by excluding obscenity from First Amendment protection. Libel and slander have never enjoyed First Amendment protection. "Fighting" words, calculated to arouse anger and immediate reaction, are similarly unprotected. So too was purely commercial speech, that is, advertising and the like, until recently. In all of these situations, no political purpose was evident, and the Court had little difficulty in holding, on the implicit basis that no positive liberty was involved, that the types of speech should receive no protection.

But a competing interpretation of the First Amendment, premised on negative liberty considerations, does exist. Professor Thomas I. Emerson, one of our most eminent

First Amendment scholars, believes that the First Amendment also serves the goals of individual self-fulfillment and the discovery of truth, independent of their relationship to the governing process. Justices Black and Douglas, perhaps more so than any other recent members of the Court, came to view the First Amendment as setting up an inviolable shield for any type of speech, regardless of its link to politics or not. For them obscenity was protected, as was libel. Their individual opinions over the course of their judicial careers bear witness to the negative liberty component they found in the First Amendment.

Looking at the cases over time, one can discern a trend in which the positive notion of liberty is being expanded so as to provide the same First Amendment protection that would have resulted from a negative notion of liberty. The key to this expansion is the broadening of the concept of self-government beyond a narrowly defined political sphere to include the general conduct of one's life. Once self-government is viewed so expansively, the realm of information necessary for self-government greatly increases. We can now understand better why the Court in 1966 said the First Amendment "is not the preserve of political expression or comment on public affairs." This trend explains at least some of the apparent inconsistencies in the cases and justifies developments in the fields of libel, privacy, and commercial speech.

Since political speech no longer monopolized the First Amendment, other speech received explicit protection. One case noted that the First Amendment provides citizens with "access to social, political, esthetic, moral and other ideas and experiences." In the 1973 obscenity trilogy, the Court said the First Amendment protected "genuine, serious literary, artistic, political or scientific expression." Perhaps this is all a homecoming to Justice Holmes' familiar explanation of the First Amendment in terms of "free trade in ideas." In any event, after leaving its moorings to political speech, the Supreme Court unsurprisingly held commercial speech protected on the ground that citizens need a free flow of such information in order to make decisions in their daily lives, indeed, that a citizen's interest in such information "may be as keen, if not keener by far, than his interest in the day's most urgent political debate."

Such a perceptible trend should not, however, obscure the fact that tensions and conflicts exist in the First Amendment field and that many of them are attributable to the tension and conflicts between negative and positive liberty. A trend in decision does not allow us to mask the fact that choices must be made and that we cannot evade what Berlin calls the "agony of choice." There is a tendency in judicial opinions to show an apparently harmonious and all-embracing resolution of a question, even when such harmony and comprehensiveness do not really exist. A sonorous formula may in fact be, as Felix Frankfurter pointed out, a "euphemistic disguise for an unresolved conflict." We should be careful not to be misled by the soothing language and seemingly irresistible logic of judicial opinions into thinking that the Court is not making hard choices.

Choice in the First Amendment field is often between rights and other rights; not power versus rights but rights versus rights. It is not always a conflict between governmental power and individual rights, though such conflicts exist. Rather the choice many times is between the positive liberty interest in free speech or press, on the one hand, and some countervailing negative liberty interest, on the other. The inevitability of such choice becomes clear in the context of a few intractable constitutional problems.

The positive liberty interest in free speech often collides, for example, with the negative liberty interests of the potential audience and the surrounding community. That audience, which may be involuntary, has valid negative liberty claims to privacy, peace and quiet, to not be offended, disturbed, annoyed, to be let alone.

The negative liberty interest of the owner of the property on which the freedom of expression is being exercised can be a difficult problem. Where the property is privately owned, even where it is a business open to the public, the property owner's negative liberty interest in trespass laws has prevailed, on the theory that, "The right to freedom of expression is a right to express views—not a right to force other people to supply a platform or a pulpit." Decision is closer where the public has unrestricted access to the private property, or where the private property has been dedicated to the public.

A classic confrontation is posed by the libel and invasion of privacy cases. There the positive liberty interest in freedom of the press is pitted against the negative liberty interest in an individual preserving his reputation unimpaired or his privacy uninvaded.

The administration of criminal justice necessitates choosing between positive and negative liberty. In the fair trial-free press context, the defendant's negative liberty interest embodied in his right to a fair trial runs up against the positive liberty interest in allowing the press to inform the public of the trial. Although the Supreme Court has shied away from actual prior restraints on press coverage of trials, it has taken great pains to ensure the inviolability of the trial's fairness, sometimes going so far as to require recalcitrant newsmen to turn over their working papers where they might benefit a criminal defendant.

Related to the fair trial-free press problem is the thorny question of whether the press can be excluded from a criminal trial. In 1979, the Supreme Court held that the Sixth Amendment right to a public trial was a right personal to the accused (a negative liberty), conferring no right of access to pretrial proceedings by the public or the press (a positive liberty). A year later, the same Court held that the First Amendment, of its own force and as applied to the states through the Fourteenth Amendment, secures the public an independent right of access to trial proceedings (a positive liberty). Explaining the different outcomes of these decisions is not easy, but at least they are comprehensible as choices between positive and negative liberty.

Choice between positive and negative liberty is one type of choice, but not the only one in First Amendment cases. Another kind of choice is seen in the Court's continuing to view obscenity as beyond the First Amendment. The Court has made a conscious choice, rightly or wrongly, that obscenity has nothing to offer even the constitutionally protected need for unimpeded flow of ideas and information for self-governance broadly defined. It has rejected the negative liberty argument advanced to protect obscenity. Deep forces are at work in such a decision, for, as Berlin writes:

"To protest against the laws governing censorship or personal morals as intolerable infringements of personal liberty presupposes a belief that the activities which such laws forbid are fundamental needs of men as men, in a good (or, indeed, any) society. To defend such laws is to hold that these needs are not essential, or that they cannot be satisfied without sacrificing other values which come higher—satisfy deeper needs—than individual freedom, determined by some standard that is not merely subjective, a standard for which some objective status—*empirical* or *a priori*—is claimed."

The rationales given by the Supreme Court in obscenity cases fit this description, for they all exude the notion that protecting obscenity would sacrifice to individual freedom certain values implicit in the Justices' concept of man, tone of society, and the good life, values felt by the Court to take precedence over individual liberty in this particular instance. If the choice causes problems for constitutional theory, it is the theory that needs to be revised. Realizing the basic and difficult choice being made, we perhaps can be more understanding if symmetry and logic are sometimes lacking, particularly where the irrational elements of sexuality may be involved.

In each of these cases, and countless others, the Court chooses between positive and negative liberty as each relates to the Free Speech and Press Clauses. Despite the related tendencies to downplay the act of choice and to synthesize individual choices into a comprehensive theory, there is no responsible way to avoid the necessity to make the difficult choices. It is as if Berlin is right that somehow we feel unhappy that a choice between ultimate values need even be made. But choose we must, and the choice depends, in the last analysis, as Berlin points out, "on our moral, religious, intellectual, economic, and aesthetic values; which are, in their turn, bound up with our conception of man, of the basic demands of his nature. In other words, our solution of such problems is based on our vision, by which we are consciously or unconsciously guided, of what constitutes a fulfilled human life." By frankly recognizing the need for such choice between positive and negative freedom, as well as the basis for choosing, we are acting out Berlin's theory in the realm of the Speech and Press Clauses.

Like the rights of free speech and press, the First Amendment rights relating to assembly, petition, and association also have primarily positive liberty components. As is practically obvious from the very wording of the pertinent language of the Amendment—"Congress shall make no law . . . abridging . . . the right of the people peaceably to assemble, and to petition the government for a redress of grievances"—the Framers intended those rights to guarantee unimpeded lines of communication between citizens and government. Their essence is not so much the right of the individual to do what he wants without interference (although that is an aspect), as it is to ensure the individual certain political rights and to facilitate his freedom of expression in that regard. The rights of assembly, petition, and association guarantee that citizens will not be deprived of certain forms of political participation.

As might be expected, application and interpretation of the rights of assembly, petition, and association present many of the same basic types of hard choices between positive and negative liberty posed by the Speech and Press Clauses. By far the most common collision is between the positive liberty interest in assembly and petition and the negative liberty interest on the part of government and the public in general. This tension, and the difficulties in dealing with it, emerged quite clearly during the civil rights movement of the 1960s. When cases arose involving civil rights demonstrations on city streets, near courthouses or jails, the Supreme Court, in reviewing convictions for disturbing the peace or trespass, identified the issue in terms of the competing interests along positive and negative liberty lines.

To frame the issue thus is to lay bare the inevitability of choice. Again and again the Court explained that freedom of expression and the ancient use of public places for assembly and discussion is only half the equation; that there was a legitimate interest in regulating the use of streets and other facilities to assure the safety and convenience of people in their use, that their public convenience must be taken into account in the interest of all. This group of cases, though perhaps couched in terms of time, place, and manner restrictions, is marked by strong language and sharp division among the Justices, reflecting differing values ascribed to the competing positive and negative liberty interests.

A more subtle but increasingly more important and more common conflict between positive and negative liberty occurs when persons exercise the right of petition to approach courts, legislatures, executive officials, zoning boards and the like for the purpose of injuring other persons or hampering competitors. There the First Amendment activity may be a cloak for ulterior motives that, to put it mildly, do not rise to the dignity of traditional First Amendment activity. In such a case, the competitor's negative liberty interest in being free of predatory and anticompetitive conduct outweighs the positive liberty interest in the right of petition. Similarly, the common law actions for malicious prosecution and abuse of process embody a balancing of the positive liberty interest in access to the courts and the negative liberty interest in individuals not being sued without cause.

Is the First Amendment a positive or negative liberty provision? The question is hard to answer. In the first place, the Amendment encompasses several provisions, not all of them designed for the same end. In the second place, the question as phrased may be too simplistic because it fails to take account of the possibility that a single constitutional provision may well be Janus-faced, and point two ways at the same time, without doing violence to its intended purpose. But enough evidence and analysis are available to offer certain conclusions.

The relevant factors at least suggest, quite strongly, that the protections in the First Amendment, with the exception of certain aspects of Religion Clauses, were all designed primarily to promote positive liberty. A close relationship exists between the rights of assembly and petition, on the one hand, and free speech and press, on the other. That the Framers put them in the same amendment is highly instructive. The positive liberty attributes of the rights of assembly, petition and association bear on the scope of the Speech and Press Clauses. To be sure, even now debate exists about whether freedom of speech and press protects only political speech. To conclude that the First Amendment is a primarily positive liberty provision is consistent with the generally accepted proposition that the main purpose of the First Amendment protection for speech and press was to insulate political speech.

But the issue is more complicated than that. The first objection to concluding that only political speech is protected stems from the language of the Amendment itself, which on its face is not limited to political speech. Some weight, after all, must be given to the text. The second problem is that difficulties would arise in defining political as opposed to nonpolitical speech. Thirdly, some evidence exists to show that at the time the Amendment was passed freedom of speech and press meant much more than political speech. Finally, and probably most importantly, the First Amendment has been interpreted over the course of time to protect nonpolitical speech as well.

These problems make it difficult to choose either an exclusively positive or negative liberty interpretation of the Speech and Press Clauses. The result, which should not be all that surprising, is that at times tensions will arise from an interpretation that includes the opposite pulls of the two concepts of liberty. The only way to avoid such tensions is to pick one type of liberty at the expense of another, which two hundred years of history and emotional attachment will not let us do, regardless of the ultimate facts. But if it is too late in the day to argue that only political speech deserves protection, at least it is always timely to expect that considerations of intent and structure inform decisions in new contexts. If positive liberty was originally the overriding goal of freedom of speech and press—and there seems to be little disagreement about that—then that goal has an important role to play in mapping the outer reaches of the First Amendment.

IV

Not only does Berlin's theory help us understand First Amendment and non-First Amendment freedoms as separate groups, but it also improves comprehension of the relationship between First Amendment freedoms and other basic freedoms. Against the conceptual background of negative and positive liberty, the relationship between competing rights takes on larger meaning.

The First Amendment is sometimes treated more gingerly than other basic liberties. There are, for instance, references in Supreme Court opinions to the "preferred position" of freedom of speech. This so-called preferred-position doctrine requires courts to scrutinize more carefully laws in the First Amendment area than in other areas. It is based on the assumption that exercise of First Amendment freedoms is the primary means by which political change occurs, that restricting First Amendment freedoms will make it more difficult to effect change relating to other freedoms, and, conversely, that encouraging First Amendment freedoms will bring about changes relating to other freedoms.

The preferred-position doctrine is in essence an elevation of positive freedom over negative freedom. The preferred-position doctrine is not really limited to the First Amendment but extends to curtailment of the political processes generally, and unmistakably puts greater value on positive liberty over negative liberty. The conclusion seems inescapable that the Supreme Court has occasionally thought positive liberty more valuable and worthy of protection than negative liberty.

The preferred-position doctrine, of course, represents a choice in favor of positive liberty. Such a choice once again exposes the tension that sometimes arises between positive and negative liberty, and, in a larger sense, uncovers the problem of harmonizing apparently incompatible values. But the threshold inquiry is perhaps addressed to whether or not any conflict or tension exists requiring a choice.

Assuming a choice must be made, is it so clear that positive liberty is entitled—as the preferred-position theory entitles it—to more protection than negative liberty? As an abstract matter, we know that both senses of liberty are important. But Berlin himself explains how both forms of freedom may take second place to even more elementary needs:

"It is true that to offer political rights, or safeguards against intervention by the state, to men who are half-naked, illiterate, underfed and diseased is to mock their condition; they need medical help or education before they can understand or make use of, an increase in their freedom. What is freedom to those who cannot make use of it? Without adequate conditions for the use of freedom what is the value of freedom?"

Yet many of these basic needs—without which positive and negative liberty are meaningless—are not considered fundamental enough by the Supreme Court to warrant special treatment under the Constitution. The Court thinks they are important, yes, but not so fundamental as to justify, under the Equal Protection Clause, imposing strict scrutiny of laws that classify or restrict on the basis of such needs. This somewhat bizarre state of affairs has been explained by viewing such basic needs as part of the distributional system whose benefits are not directly essential to political participation. Courts, according to the explanation, are right in viewing the results of the distributional process as irrelevant or gratuitous. Any maldistribution, continues the argument, ultimately depends on the political process with which courts are more properly concerned.

Once the most basic needs are met or facilely brushed aside, the choice arises. The text of the Bill of Rights does not appear to make the choice. On the contrary, each of the first eight amendments reads as a specific prohibition on governmental power, without any statement that one amendment is more valuable than any other. Nor is the legislative intent behind the Bill of Rights appreciably more enlightening. The legislative history amply demonstrates that *all* the amendments were necessary for passage. To draw distinctions between the importance of individual amendments is to indulge our own notions of what we think is important.

The structure of the Constitution has led some astute observers to discern a governmental plan with special stress on positive freedom. In his book *Democracy and Distrust,* Professor John Hart Ely concludes that the Constitution consists primarily of provisions dealing with structure and "process" in the political sense and in the more narrow sense of dispute resolution. Aside from the concern with structure and process, according to Ely, substantive values are few and far between and, in the main, conspicuously absent from the Constitution. From this apparent focus on process rather than substantive values, one could perhaps infer that provisions like the First Amendment, which play such a crucial role in the political process, are entitled to greater respect than other provisions. The flaw in this argument is that it ascribes comparative importance to positive freedom without taking into account the equally crucial importance of negative freedom.

To expose this flaw, we merely need to examine the function of certain other amendments bearing on negative liberty. What Ely describes as "process writ small" is the catalogue of procedures required in a criminal trial. The Bill of Rights' concern with this aspect of "process" is pronounced. Can there be any doubt that a defendant in a criminal trial would view these constitutionally mandated procedural safeguards as more protective of his liberty than an abstract right to free expression? Or, outside the criminal procedure field, could we seriously question that a person whose property has been condemned will put more faith in the Fifth Amendment prohibition against takings without just compensation than he would in the impact of his First Amendment rights?

In fact the preferred-position doctrine follows no coherent pattern. Generally speaking, legislation or regulation concerning *social* or *economic* matters is judged by a "rational basis" test. This test is the weakest possible, for it means the legislation or regulation is valid unless it can be shown to be irrational and unrelated to its stated purpose. So far so good, in terms of conventional preferred-position theory. But more severe tests—often called "strict scrutiny"—are used for other types of legislation having nothing to do with positive freedom. In the celebrated

Bakke affirmative action case, the opinion by Justice Powell even went so far as to apply the "strict scrutiny" test to a classification disadvantaging a *majority* group. Hence, other concepts besides positive liberty enjoy a preferred position, thereby making application of the preferred-position doctrine inconsistent.

The ultimate defect in preferred-position theory is its anti-democratic cast. If the Constitution enshrines a system of political process based on popular decisions—positive liberty—are we not regressing by imposing subjective value judgments on those decisions? To assert that freedom of expression, or some other freedom, is *the* most important right is to adopt a rather elitist position. The assertion turns on what any particular individual, group, judge, or commentator views as important or fundamental. History shows us that people differ on such issues.

Intellectual fashion may have a lot to do with what particular type of liberty is preferred at a particular time. Indeed, it may well be that the ultimate value is negative liberty which thrives better in a system of positive liberty. Some evidence exists to support the view that the people who wrote the Constitution thought that way. As Isaiah Berlin himself notes: "Perhaps the chief value of political—positive—rights, of participating in the government, is as a means for protecting what they hold to be an ultimate value, namely individual—negative—liberty." Certainly, the Supreme Court's performance during the heyday of substantive due process showed that it thought negative liberty concepts like "liberty of contract" deserved more protection than positive freedoms.

The defects in preferred-position theory do not mean that we can or should avoid choosing between positive and negative liberty. But they do serve as a cautionary tale about the consequences of our choice.

V

If the preferred-position doctrine elevates positive freedom, then the institution of judicial review denigrates such
liberty, at least to some extent. For the basic function of
judicial review is that a court overrides the political processes. An unelected body prevents the elected branches
from governing as they wish. Such a power is difficult to
reconcile with the underlying democratic assumptions of
our system. Insofar as judicial review is incompatible with
democratic theory, it is in tension with positive liberty.

This tension between judicial review and positive liberty
is not substantially reduced by the familiar argument that
in applying the Constitution judges are simply applying the
people's will. According to that argument, since the "people" ratified the Constitution, the "people" are responsible
for judicial review. Thus the judges do not check the people, the argument continues, the Constitution does, which
means the "people" in the last analysis are checking themselves. But this argument, despite its impressive lineage
and widespread acceptance, is "largely a fake." Court cases
turn on constitutional language that in no reasonable way
reflects the feelings of a contemporary majority, but rather
express the feelings of persons long since gone from the
scene.

Precisely because the basic problem of judicial review is
its conflict with democratic theory, the extensive literature
cannot avoid discussing the subject in terms of political
rights, that is, positive liberty. Indeed, one of the doctrines
by which courts claim to steer clear of the conflict—the
"political question" doctrine—bears in its very name and
substance an open acknowledgment that the judiciary
should be wary of overriding the political process. Yet
few—if any—would do away entirely with judicial review,

despite its inherent tension with majority rule. From the start, Americans were aware that a majority in power would have the potential for tyrannizing or otherwise taking advantage of the minority. Although judicial review serves as a means of protecting minorities from majority tyranny, it is instructive to see clearly what specific goals will justify courts overruling positive liberty expressed by the political process.

The goal of judicial review most consistent with democratic theory and positive liberty is, not surprisingly, more positive liberty. Thus courts have intervened in reapportionment cases and voting rights cases in which the ordinary political processes had resulted in persons being excluded from or significantly limited in participating in those very political processes. The same rationale justifies judicial review where the political processes inhibit the mechanisms for political change by restricting freedom of expression. Focusing on the compatibility of this facet of judicial review and what we have referred to as positive liberty, John Hart Ely has tellingly argued that "a representation-reinforcing approach to judicial review [is] . . . entirely supportive of the underlying premises of the American system of representative democracy." In essence, this position means that judicial review is appropriate to override the political process for the purpose of policing the process of representation and clearing the channels of political change. Courts can interfere with positive liberty if the goal is a truer conception of positive liberty.

But American judicial history also contains many instances of judicial review where the political process restricted negative liberty. Whether we approve of them or not, the cases decided under the flag of substantive due process clearly represent judicial review in the service of what the courts deemed individual liberty. In language resembling Berlin's language, the Supreme Court in 1900 said:

The liberty mentioned in that amendment [i.e., the Fourteenth] means not only the right of the citizen to be free from the mere physical restraint of his person, as by incarceration, but the term is deemed to embrace the right of the citizen to be free in the enjoyment of all his faculties; to be free to use them in all lawful ways; to live and work where he will; to earn his livelihood by any lawful calling; to pursue any livelihood or avocation, and for that purpose to enter into all contracts which may be proper, necessary and essential to his carrying out to a successful conclusion the purposes above mentioned.

Although conventional wisdom and several Supreme Court opinions have noted the passing of substantive due process, the fact is that it has surfaced again explicitly in the abortion cases and implicitly in cases decided under the Equal Protection Clause of the Fourteenth Amendment. Nor can we overlook cases where the courts have voided legislative or executive actions violating specific negative liberty provisions in the Constitution, be they concerned with the free exercise of religion, criminal procedural safeguards, bills of attainder, ex post facto laws, contractual obligations, or the like.

Positive and negative liberty are not the only justification for judicial review. The Constitution includes many provisions either structural or "housekeeping" in nature. If the political process produces a law violating such a provision, a court should properly void the law as inconsistent with the organic document of government. For example, if a state passes a law violating the Commerce Clause, or Congress or the President exceeds the powers granted by the Constitution, a court could nullify the law even though it has no apparent relationship to positive or negative liberty. But there is little that is controversial in this context, especially where it is state legislation under review.

The several reasons for invoking judicial review uncover an interesting relationship between judicial review and the preferred-position doctrine. Preferred-position theory requires stricter scrutiny of actions restricting positive liberty; but judicial review is in tension with the end results of the normal exercise of those very same political liberties; so judicial review has as one of its key justifications the refereeing of positive liberty. A surface incongruity appears in reapportionment cases that used the lowest common denominator test of "irrationality" rather than a stricter test (arguably called for under preferred-position theory) in evaluating the governmental actions under scrutiny. Although reliance on the weak "rational basis" test seems inconsistent with the supposedly special solicitude due positive liberty, the fact is that what the Court said was not what it did. Its actions, if not its words, were fully compatible with the underlying theory. From this point of view, the preferred-position doctrine and judicial review are flipsides of the same constitutional coin.

Judicial review represents a crucial area where we cannot evade the "necessity and agony of choice." Professor Lawrence Tribe tells us: "There is simply no way for courts to review legislation in terms of the Constitution without repeatedly making difficult substantive choices among competing values, and indeed among inevitably controverted political, social, and moral conceptions." An important school of thought believes that the Supreme Court is exactly the institution that should discover, define, evolve, proclaim, and apply fundamental values for our society. Surely this concept of judicial review exemplifies the thrust of Berlin's teaching about the inevitability of choice.

The value-choosing function of judicial review, however, has come under severe attack. The main objection is that the values chosen ultimately are the judge's own values, despite attempts to describe them as objective or impersonal. For judicial review to be based on a judge imposing his own values has an essentially anti-democratic character. This is the reason why Ely argues for a representation-reinforcing theory of judicial review as opposed to a value-protective theory. Ely would favor the elimination of the value-choosing function of judicial review.

But even Ely's theory fails to eliminate entirely the necessity of choice. At most it reduces the scope of choice. Ely is an "interpretivist," who confines judges to enforcing norms stated or clearly implied in the written Constitution, and differs from "noninterpretivists," who encourage judges to go beyond that set of references and enforce norms not discoverable in the Constitution. The difference between them depends on where the values are derived from. Although "noninterpretivism" chooses values not discoverable in the Constitution, "interpretivism" still requires the exercise of choice between values in the Constitution, particularly in connection with open-ended clauses that invite such interpretation. Neither "noninterpretivism" nor "interpretivism" can escape a choice of values where two constitutional rights collide, for example, fair trial and free press. Choices, and terribly important ones at that, are therefore quite necessary even in the interpretivist's universe.

Perhaps the tension between judicial review and democratic theory can never be resolved completely. Of course the tension here is not simply a conflict between positive and negative liberty. Other things are involved. Even so, Berlin's comments about the inevitability of choice are highly relevant. For Berlin was not limiting himself to conflicts between his two concepts of liberty. He perceived conflict between values as something broader, something inherent in the human condition.

VI

Studying constitutional law in light of the two concepts of liberty yields significant results. At its simplest level, it organizes and classifies constitutional liberties as positive or negative, or, rarely, both. It helps define the scope and meaning of First Amendment rights and other rights. It calls into question the preferred-position doctrine. It explains judicial review from a new perspective. Reliance on the two concepts of liberty provides an overlay on the cases, an unmasking of the dynamics of the case-law development with its sometimes inconsistent outcomes.

The most significant result of all is the astounding and melancholy revelation that irreconcilable tension exists between the two concepts of liberty and that choosing between those concepts is a basic and unavoidable fact in much of constitutional law. This means nothing less than that the most fundamental twin premises of constitutional liberty are at times inconsistent. In deciding constitutional cases, therefore, courts cannot simultaneously realize positive and negative liberty. One or the other must yield; choice—awfully difficult choice—is inevitable.

In identifying this inevitable tension and choice lies the originality of Isaiah Berlin for constitutional law. To be sure, Berlin himself did not work out how this great insight applies to constitutional law. But he pointed the way, he was the first to see the basic conflict, making it relatively easy to accomplish the task of actually unpacking constitutional law with Berlin's insight in mind. In this respect, Berlin resembles one of his heroes, Machiavelli.

Against the Current, the third volume of Berlin's collected essays, contains a piece entitled "The Originality of Machiavelli," in which Berlin describes Machiavelli's "cardinal achievement" as his uncovering the "uncomfortable truth" that "ends equally ultimate, equally sacred, may contradict each other." This achievement "is of the first order" because it undermines "the central current of Western thought," which is that there exists some single principle, a single harmonious whole, a single intelligible structure, a unifying monistic pattern, a single universal overarching standard, an infallible measuring rod to enable man to choose rationally between competing ends. Machiavelli's "profoundly upsetting conclusion" is no more upsetting than Berlin's: both compel man to choose between goals that "are not merely in practice, but in principle incompatible." It was Berlin who uncovered this dilemma in connection with positive and negative liberty.

Once lawyers realize or even glimpse the implications of Berlin's theory for constitutional law, the most visible outcome should be a revised style of discourse in constitutional law. Many questions of constitutional law will then be explicitly cast in terms of choosing between positive and negative liberty. Explicitly identifying the competing values and making the choice explicit should enhance the rationality as well as the clarity and intellectual honesty of constitutional decisionmaking. "If adjudication is to be a rational process," Justice Frankfurter said in another context, "we cannot escape a candid examination of the conflicting claims with full recognition that both are supported by weighty title-deeds."

The implications of Berlin's epoch-making argument are constructive. They introduce into the foundations of constitutional law a new and fertile technique of analysis. If the dilemma of choice remains unresolved, Berlin's essay can at least teach constitutional law to live with it. If collisions between positive and negative liberty are not seen as rare, exceptional, and disastrous, then perhaps the act of choice will become less agonizing.

Apart from positive and negative liberty, constitutional law involves two other fundamental concepts—federalism and separation of powers—that operate in terms of the overall superstructure of our form of government. Federalism embodies the tension between a national government, on the one hand, and state governments, on the other. It is at the root of decisions about state regulation and national economy, the scope of the Commerce Clause, congressional ordering of federal-state relationships, state taxation and free trade, and intergovernmental immunities and interstate relationships. The separation of powers deals with tensions between the different branches of the national government. It explains decisions involving checks and balances, the scope and conflict between the powers of the three branches, congressional power, presidential power, and judicial power.

These four concepts—positive liberty, negative liberty, federalism, and separation of powers—may point the way to a master theory of constitutional law. Every constitutional provision can be grouped under one of these heads. Every constitutional problem can be formulated as a problem involving these concepts, either in isolation or in the context of tensions between them. Exceptions do not readily come to mind. Indeed, identifying the concepts involved should facilitate identifying the competing policy considerations implicated by any problem of constitutional law.

It would be a supreme irony if Berlin's theory led to a unified theory of constitutional law. Such a master theory resembles the type of monism repudiated by Berlin. Yet the possibility calls for further thought and study. There may be deep but hidden connections between the basic concepts of constitutional law.

Applying Berlin's essay "Two Concepts of Liberty" to constitutional law should not be construed as an invitation to despair. The discovery that constitutional law is founded and practiced within a set of tensions between aims not simultaneously realizable in full does not mean that chaos must prevail. It does mean that we frequently must choose, and we must know what we want, and be ready to pay the price. Nor does the fact that we cannot explain all constitutional phenomena in terms of a single underlying theory entail any lessening of freedom, positive or negative. On the contrary, when one ideal is the only goal, that goal inevitably requires the sacrifice of other ideals; pluralism, recognizing the diversity and rivalry of human goals, produces toleration and compromise, skepticism and doubt, all of which lead to more, not less, liberty.

2

The Supreme Court and the New Formalism

It is not often that a popular book about the Supreme Court makes it appropriate to reevaluate the nature of law and legal philosophy. Yet that is exactly the legacy of *The Brethren* by Bob Woodward and Scott Armstrong. *The Brethren* was the first full-length book devoted to reporting—ostensibly from the viewpoint of a fly on the walls of the Justices' conference room and chambers—the Supreme Court's decisionmaking process, warts and all. Ever since the Supreme Court's beginnings, the inner workings of its decisionmaking process have for the most part been shrouded in secrecy. In the past, we have caught only brief, occasional behind-the-scenes glimpses, usually given by Justices themselves in the form of law review articles or posthumously published letters, diaries, or private memoranda. But the revelations in *The Brethren* made it a best seller. Rarely has a book about law sparked such wide interest both inside and outside the profession.

When *The Brethren* was published in 1979, most discussions of it dwelled on the rather obvious. They highlighted its titillating nature, making it resemble a peep show with the Justices of the Supreme Court playing the lead roles. They challenged the accuracy of its facts and the use of unidentified confidential sources. They objected to the authors' imputation and interpolation of Justices' thoughts. Perhaps most serious of all, they raised basic questions about the ethics of obtaining confidential information from former law clerks. All of these points are interesting and worth noting, but still overlook other, deeper issues raised by *The Brethren*.

The central and lasting importance of *The Brethren* is its ability to show the continued potency or resurrection of a concept of the judicial process thought to be in eclipse for at least fifty years. *The Brethren* breathed new life into the doctrine that judges ought merely to "find" and "announce" rather than "make" the law, or at least rather than "make" the law as crudely and blatantly as depicted in the book.

This importance is brought into focus more by reaction to the book than by the book itself. Many commentators and reviewers of *The Brethren* said at the time that its publication would hurt the prestige of the Supreme Court. The commentators were really saying that lifting even a corner of the veil on the Supreme Court's decision-making process will damage the Court's reputation and reduce respect for its pronouncements. Presumably, they thought it would be better if the Court's decision-making process remained hidden and confidential, as it has been in the past.

But why? What is wrong with all of us learning that the Court reaches decisions by compromise? That Justices, like legislators, engage in logrolling? That decisions depend heavily on the personalities of the individual Justices rather than some abstract concept of law? Such revelations, according to the commentators, lower the Court's standing and make empty rhetoric of the adage that we are a government of laws, not of men.

As a preliminary matter, it is hard to see exactly why the

Supreme Court is so special, so unique with respect to its internal secrets. The other two branches, no less than the judiciary, are responsible for the laws of this nation, and we have become accustomed to revelations about presidential and legislative decisionmaking. Indeed, it was the Supreme Court itself, in two cases discussed at length in *The Brethren*, that refused to halt publication of a confidential study of executive decisions leading up to the Vietnam War and that substantially narrowed a recent President's claim of executive privilege with respect to confidential tapes sought by a government prosecutor. If publicity serves as an important function regarding the two branches of government subject to election, it would seem that publicity should be an even more needed external check on judges who do not stand for election but who are protected by life tenure.

Even so, there is a reluctance to subject the judiciary, particularly the Supreme Court, to the same public scrutiny as the other branches of government. A majority of a committee of The Association of the Bar of the City of New York recommended a new federal law to give the public ownership of almost all governmental records except those of federal judges. The bar association committee thought that papers of ex-federal judges were somehow different from papers of ex-Presidents, ex-presidential assistants, and ex-legislators. Inasmuch as no principled distinction can be drawn in terms of national security or other recognizable interest in confidentiality, one suspects the committee, practicing lawyers all, acted subconsciously to protect its own preserve, the courts. A similar committee composed of legislative or presidential assistants might reflect its own bias, but still the bar committee's action is symptomatic of a certain hesitancy to direct the gaze of publicity on the judicial process.

The book reviewers and the bar association are acting on the same premise. Animating them all is the sense that there is something mysterious and mystical about the way judges decide cases, something better left a secret of the initiated alone. By recoiling from public exposure of judicial decisionmaking, they are actually stirring the embers of a once fiery debate over the judicial function. Whether conscious or not, public reaction to *The Brethren* shows the profound dualism of our most basic attitudes toward law. Such a reaction counsels against a simplistic approach that often tends to view the judicial function either as a model of pure Olympian legal decisions or as a bunch of crass, willful, and arbitrary rulings.

There is no blinking the fact that public reaction to *The Brethren* in some respects harks back to the jurisprudence of an earlier era. Between the Civil War and World War I, the legal profession in America viewed law as fixed for all time and invested with almost supernatural authority. The prevailing philosophy of the judicial function was that judges found and declared what the law was; they did not make law. Law, like truth, was seen as something transcendental, immutable and eternal, part of a closed, logical system that could meet any fact pattern by the use of deductive reasoning. Judges were no more than vessels through which the law spoke. A judge's duty was simply to "discover" and "announce" the true law that had always been floating around somewhere.

Such formalism made it appear as if law was something more than man-made. Judges rarely explained the reasons for their decisions. It was thought sufficient simply for a court to state that the rule being applied had long been settled and then list a string of precedents without discussion. "Indeed," as Professor Grant Gilmore has pointed out, "it was improper, unfitting, unjudicial to say more." The predominant style of judging helped hide from the legal community, let alone the public, any other reality in the making of judicial decisions.

Although formalism held sway for a time, it had its critics. As early as 1880, the great Oliver Wendell Holmes, Jr. published his lectures on *The Common Law* in which he wrote these familiar but classic lines:

"The life of the law has not been logic; it has been experience. The felt necessities of the time, the prevalent moral and political theories, intuitions of public policy, avowed or unconscious, even the prejudices which judges share with their fellow-men, have had a good deal more to do than the syllogism in determining the rules by which men should be governed."

As a judge, Holmes frankly said that judges do legislate; they do make law. This attitude became the central theme of *The Nature of the Judicial Process,* a series of lectures delivered by Benjamin Cardozo in 1920. Yet, so entrenched was formalism that Cardozo's suggestion that judges were more than slot machines—that judges made law rather than merely announced it—caused a furor.

Inspired by Holmes and Cardozo, a movement known as Legal Realism grew up in the 1920s and '30s. Legal Realism was skeptical of conventional theories of formalism. In a series of writings, men like Karl Llewellyn and Jerome Frank showed that the widespread notion that law either is or can be predictable or certain is an illusion or myth. They ridiculed what philosopher Morris R. Cohen called "the phonographic theory of the judicial function," the view that judges do not make and change law. They advocated the use of sociological facts and empirical research to justify the social policies or sets of values or goals on which judicial decisions rested.

By the end of the 1930s, Legal Realism seemed to have

swept the field. Its once revolutionary notions have themselves become received wisdom. Judges, practitioners, professors, and the public have all accepted the concept of
judge-made law. Legal Realism's victory was so complete
that now any contrary idea tends to strike us, sophisticated
as we think we are, as immature. Jurisprudential debate no
longer revolves around whether or not judges make the
law. That debate is over, or so it seemed until publication
of *The Brethren.*

The Brethren makes us reconsider that debate. By arguing that exposure of the Supreme Court's decisionmaking
process hurts the prestige of the Court, reviewers of *The
Brethren* are in effect resurrecting a debate most within the
profession had assumed was over. Not only are such commentators reviving the debate, but they are also making us
all question whether the debate in fact ever ended or is
capable of ending. Their fear that publicity of the Court's
actual deliberative process diminishes respect for the Court
at once belies the completeness of Legal Realism's victory
and shows the continuing vitality of at least some aspects
of the old formalist jurisprudence. It points the way to a
new synthetic jurisprudence that, by avoiding either extreme, is more true to the facts.

The neo-formalism expressed by reviewers of *The Brethren* has its attractiveness. It is comforting to believe that
the law is certain and predictable, and not subject to alteration by judges who are, after all, ordinary mortals. Law
then takes on an aspect of the supernatural, which, as an
instrument of social engineering, is an effective quality. In
this sense, formalism and religion have much in common.
A major source of strength for both is the notion that the
rules being applied are handed down from a higher authority than man-made institutions. This notion is consciously enhanced by the usually grand and impressive

architectural style of houses of worship and courthouses, by vestments for priests and black robes for judges, and by dramatic use of ritual and formalized jargon.

But the root cause of formalism's continued attractiveness lies deeper. In *Law and the Modern Mind,* published in 1930, Jerome Frank convincingly argued that the wellspring of legal formalism was psychological. According to Frank, adults, in trying to recapture the emotional satisfaction of their childhood, without being consciously aware of their motivation, seek in their legal systems the authoritativeness, certainty and predictability that the child believed he or she had found in the law laid down by the father. Frank modestly considered this a partial explanation for the myth of certainty in the law. More than fifty years later, we still can appreciate the insight of Frank's analysis.

Given the underlying reasons for the attractiveness of formalism, it is not surprising that formalism has some appeal in all eras. These underlying reasons are too intertwined with human nature and psychology to disappear just because they are recognized. For that recognition, we have Legal Realism to thank. But Legal Realism, no matter how much lip service we pay to it, did not change human nature, nor did it entirely wipe out formalism or formalism's attractiveness. Law is meant to apply to all people, not just law professors, and any theory of jurisprudence that ignores human nature and psychology does so at its peril. It may be that an emotionally mature mind would not need the fictions of formalism, but we must take mankind as we find it, and until drastic changes occur, many people depend on the formalist myths. Any triumph by Legal Realism, by necessity, could never be complete unless the makeup of the human mind and personality changed all of a sudden. Legal Realism, from this point of view, is unrealistic.

Rather than an either-or situation—either all formalism or all realism—any genuine jurisprudence must contain strains of both. No jurisprudential monism suffices. Whereas formalism suffers from the flaw of failing to take account of the reality of the judicial function, Legal Realism pays insufficient heed, despite its name, to the reality of human nature and psychology. A dualist jurisprudence, one that recognizes the ever present tension between formalism and Legal Realism, is more likely to reflect the truth accurately. Of course, this is not to say that in any given era one or the other component strain might not predominate.

Actually, legal history has had alternating cycles of dominant formalism and dominant realism. If Blackstone's *Commentaries* represented formalism, Bentham's efforts at codification stood for Legal Realism. If the post-Civil War period was marked by formalism in the ascendant, then the years since World War I have seen the dominance of Legal Realism. But the ability to identify alternating periods of formalism and realism fails to explain *why* a particular period should be colored by one jurisprudential strain or another. There may be social conditions more conducive to one or the other.

Is public reaction to *The Brethren* a harbinger of our entry into a new formalist era? If so, Freudian theories by themselves offer an inadequate explanation why formalism should become more visible or potent now. For an adequate explanation we might benefit from looking for similarities between the milieus in which formalism grows. After the Civil War, America was exhausted. It needed a rest. The slower rate of change during the half century after the Civil War aided the sensation that law was stable.

Could it be that similar cultural conditions now exist? Is America once again worn out? Are we as a nation spent by the convulsions and turmoil of the 1960s and '70s, by Vietnam, civil rights, student radicalism, and dishonorable conduct in high places? Is it possible that the drastic changes wrought by the Warren Court have stimulated a conservative counterrevolution not just among new Justices but among the people as well? Is it conceivable that *The Brethren*—brimming over with revelations of compromise, logrolling and in-fighting among Supreme Court Justices in their decisionmaking process—is too much to bear on top of everything else that has happened?

Perhaps the shock of *The Brethren* is simply too great for the public. We cannot blithely disregard the comments of some of our most thoughtful journalists, especially when they seem to be saying the same thing. Even if lawyers have known the truth for years, the public probably still cherishes the Supreme Court as a symbol of nine wise jurists debating the relative merits of fundamental law in a good faith effort to arrive at the one true answer. That notion must play an important role in achieving public acceptance of controversial decisions, like those concerning race relations, school prayers, and abortions. *The Brethren*, however, surely shatters whatever was left of the myth that law is certain or predictable and not blatantly made by judges on a wholesale scale. The act of shattering such a basic myth may itself cause a reaction to bolster the myth even more than before.

We should be alert to see if judicial styles and legal commentary start to bear more and more of the telltale signs of formalism. We should be careful to note the amount and type of change coming from the Supreme Court, to observe how judicial "restraint" and "activism" fare in the near future, to watch how precedents are treated. To some extent, such omens may reflect the pendulum theory of history, which is little more than a temporal application of Newtonian mechanics to society—an equal and opposite reaction to the perceived instability of a preceding era.

On the other hand, *The Brethren* may well lead to greater realism vis à vis our legal system and institutions. Truth and reality always help to wipe away the mist from our eyes. After all, it is neither shocking nor particularly offensive to learn that the judges of the highest court in the land come to their decisions not on the basis of strict legal nicety but on the basis of what they think would be best for the nation. Experienced lawyers know that precedents often exist to support both sides of a legal issue, and that ultimate decision turns on policy. Furthermore, *The Brethren* may instigate a welcome and overdue study of the Court's unwritten rules, what they are, how they function, and what happens if they are broken. It should also stimulate further interest in evaluating the performance of Supreme Court Justices. Finally the book raises serious questions about the relative virtues of lawyering as opposed to judging even at the highest level. Thus, rather than a new era of heightened formalism, we may be on the threshold of greater realism.

That *The Brethren* may simultaneously provoke formalist and realist responses only underscores the dualist nature of jurisprudence. Either way, we are in the process of change and heightened understanding. We should therefore avoid the tendency to write off *The Brethren* as mere gossip. The book highlights the complexity of the thing we call law. Its very popularity should also serve to increase its impact on legal thinking. It may even signal a turning point in American legal history, just as exposing the Wizard changed the lives of Dorothy and her friends in Oz.

3

Judicial Review

Too often we tend to think there is nothing meaningful left to say about basic things. At this late date, how much that is original or creative remains to be said about something as basic as judicial review? Have not the courts and commentators spilled enough ink on all aspects of that subject? Would it not be better to exploit the riches of a new mine, leaving alone the used-up and abandoned mine of judicial review? The answer is that we must resist succumbing to this natural tendency, and the proof is *Democracy and Distrust*, a book by John Hart Ely, the new Dean of Stanford Law School.

Democracy and Distrust, published in 1980, is the most important book about law in at least fifteen years. It is a great book, and recognizing a great book is not always easy. Sometimes there is a lot of fanfare, but the media hype frequently fails to fit the actual substance of the book. Ely's book is different; it is like Carl Sandburg's fog, which just creeps up on you. It belongs on the shelf next to Alexander Bickel's *The Least Dangerous Branch* and should be studied carefully by everyone concerned with the institution of judicial review and with constitutional law generally.

Ely's original theme is that a new theory of judicial review—what Ely calls "interpretivism"—is needed to reconcile judicial review with democratic assumptions. He finds constitutional doctrine now dominated by a "false dichotomy" between the Framers' intent and the courts as ultimate spokesmen of substantive value choices. Interpretivism requires judges deciding constitutional issues to confine themselves to enforcing norms stated or clearly implied in the written Constitution. By contrast, noninterpretivism allows courts to go beyond that set of references and enforce norms not discoverable within the Constitution. The main advantage of Ely's brand of interpretivism is that it results in a theory of judicial review more compatible with the underlying premises of our representative democracy.

Tension between judicial review and majoritarian rule is nothing new. When a court has the power to void legislation, a body not elected or otherwise politically responsible in any significant way stops the people's elected representatives from governing as they wish. Ely exposes as "largely a fake" the argument going back to Federalist No. 78 and *Marbury* v. *Madison* that judicial review was ordained by the people since *they* ratified the Constitution. But the people are not really checking themselves, because, as Ely argues, the Constitution and the amendments most frequently involved in court cases represent not the sentiment of a contemporary majority, but the voice of people dead for a century or two. Thus, the tension remains under conventional theory.

The conflict with democratic theory is exacerbated, not reduced, according to Ely, by a theory of judicial review that makes courts the source of fundamental values. Whether those values are the judges' own or referred to in more objective impersonal terms (*e.g.*, natural law, neutral principles, reason, tradition, consensus, predicting progress), there is no doubt that relying on them to override the political process has an anti-democratic cast to it. For the reality is that those so-called fundamental values, regardless of their name, are ultimately rooted in the judges' personal experience and outlook. Ely refers to the late Professor Bickel as the embodiment of the school favoring courts as discoverers of fundamental values, and *Democracy and Distrust* as a whole should be seen as a full-dress response to Bickel's *The Least Dangerous Branch*, published in 1962.

To replace Bickel's value-protective theory of judicial review, Ely proposes a representation-reinforcing approach. Ely's approach relies on the famous footnote four in the 1938 *Carolene Products* case, which suggested that stricter scrutiny should be used when courts review legislation interfering with political rights. A canvass of the Constitution convinces Ely that that document is overwhelmingly concerned with structure and process, not with substantive values, thereby ensuring broad participation in the processes and distributions of government. Ely argues that this observation should inform judicial interpretations of those open-ended constitutional provisions that invite considerations not found in their language or legislative history. Unlike value-protective theories, Ely's representation-reinforcing approach supports democratic theory and is appropriate for courts as experts on process and as political outsiders.

In short, Ely thinks courts should serve primarily as referees in policing the process of political representation. Courts should not be concerned with the particular outcomes of the political process so much as with clearing the channels of political change and facilitating the representation of minorities. This attitude requires self-control on the part of courts but not necessarily abandonment of judicial activism. As Ely points out, judicial activism and restraint cut across interpretivism and noninterpretivism. Thus, those laws that infringe on the political process are proper subjects for what is often called judicial activism.

In developing his new and exciting theory, which had to some extent been foreshadowed by his own recent law review articles, Ely spins off important insights like sparks from a generator. For instance, in almost an aside, Ely proposes an extraordinarily simple and useful method for judicial review in the free expression field. Rather than the hodgepodge of existing tests, Ely favors two complementary approaches. Where the evil the state seeks to avert is independent of the message being regulated (*e.g.*, fear of public reaction, annoyance, political assassination, etc.), Ely proposes a "specific threat" test, which includes clear and present danger as well as ad hoc balancing. Where the evil the state seeks to avert is thought to arise from the particular dangers of the message being conveyed, the courts should adopt an "unprotected messages" approach that immunizes all expression save that which falls within a few clearly and narrowly defined categories. Thus, with a flourish of his pen, Ely has developed an integrated and coherent theory of the First Amendment that does away with much present confusion.

Ely is equally penetrating on other constitutional provisions "instructing us to look beyond their four corners." He is critical of the revival of substantive due process in *Roe* v. *Wade* (the 1973 abortion case), and notes its negative feedback effect of constricting procedural due process. In analyzing the Due Process Clause of the Fourteenth Amendment, Ely explains that legislative intent in such a case is special: the views of congressmen in proposing the amendment are *not* more important than the views of those in the states voting to ratify the constitutional amendment. The Privileges or Immunities Clause of the Fourteenth Amendment strikes Ely as an underused provision meant to extend to all a set of entitlements that could well go beyond the first eight amendments. Ely convincingly disposes of the conventional reading of the Ninth Amendment—"that old constitutional jester"—as negating an inference of unenumerated powers in the Constitution. He shows that if this were so, the Tenth Amendment would be redundant. The text of the Ninth Amendment speaks of "unenumerated rights," not "powers," and there is the key for Ely.

Bringing about changes in the law is old hat for Ely. As a law student, he wrote a law review article suggesting a new approach to bills of attainder (72 Yale L.J. 330), which soon became the law of the land (*United States* v. *Brown*, 381 U.S. 437). As a summer associate, he helped Abe Fortas write the brief in *Gideon* v. *Wainwright*. As a law clerk to Chief Justice Earl Warren, Ely assisted the man perhaps most responsible for changing our public law in recent times. He also was a staff counsel to the Warren Commission on the assassination of President Kennedy. Finally, as a law professor for some fourteen years, Ely has written article after article of significance.

If *The Brethren* gave us an unsophisticated and inartful view of the Supreme Court from the inside, *Democracy and Distrust* gives us a mature, measured view from the outside, with quite as many revelations though of a different nature. Ely calls Bickel "probably the most creative constitutional theorist of the past twenty years." Ely may well be on his way to becoming the most creative constitutional theorist of the next twenty years.

4

Mr. Marbury and the All-Stars

WE UNDOUBTEDLY take too much for granted. Familiar and fundamental legal doctrines often seem to have been foreordained. Life or law without them might even be unthinkable.

But thinking the unthinkable is fun. It is also provocative. It allows us to reconsider the path of the law and to see if what is, had to be, and if there is any difference in the long run.

Take, for example, the American doctrine of judicial review. What if *Marbury* v. *Madison* had never been decided? Is judicial review such a foregone and obvious conclusion?

Pretend for a moment we are writing on a blank slate. Imagine we are a fly on the wall of the conference room of an all-star Supreme Court. Nine past justices, who in their lifetimes grappled with the problem of judicial review, discuss Marbury's suit.

John Marshall's position is no mystery. In considering whether Marbury was entitled to a writ of mandamus, Marshall perceived a clash between the Constitution and an act of Congress. The Constitution gives the Supreme Court "original jurisdiction in all cases affecting ambassadors, other public ministers and consuls, and those in which a state shall be a party. In all other cases, the Supreme Court shall have appellate jurisdiction."

But Section 13 of the Judiciary Act of 1789 purported to give the Court "power to issue . . . writs of mandamus, in cases warranted by the principles and usages of law, to any courts appointed, or persons holding office, under the authority of the United States." Such mandamus power, in Marshall's view, was part of original rather than appellate jurisdiction.

Since Marshall thought the statute's grant of power unwarranted by the Constitution, he found it necessary to ask whether an act repugnant to the Constitution can become the law of the land, and whether the Supreme Court has the power to void an act of Congress.

As the world knows, Marshall held that the Constitution, as "superior paramount law unchangeable by ordinary means," controls any legislative act repugnant to it. He concluded further that it is the "very essence of judicial duty" to decide which law—Constitution or statute—governs. In view of the perceived conflict between the Constitution and Section 13 of the Judiciary Act, Marshall found the statute void as unconstitutional.

Roger Taney, author of the *Dred Scott* decision, probably would have agreed with Marshall. If the Supreme Court could not declare an act of Congress unconstitutional, then, Taney might have said to himself, an abomination like the Missouri Compromise would be allowed to deprive slaveholders of their property. Such a deprivation could not possibly be tolerated in a free nation, Taney might have reasoned.

Stephen Field or George Sutherland might well have approached Marbury's case from a different angle. The issue for them might not have been whether the Court had the power to declare acts of Congress unconstitutional, but whether the Court would tolerate interference by government with substantive liberty.

Field and Sutherland (and several others) might have viewed the facts as an interference with Marbury's liberty guaranteed by the Due Process Clause of the Fifth Amendment. Former President John Adams had appointed Marbury to be a judge; Madison had refused to give the commission to Marbury. Therefore, Madison is infringing on Marbury's constitutional rights. For Field and Sutherland (and other subscribers to substantive due process), it might have been Madison's actions, not the act of Congress, that should have been held unconstitutional.

Oliver Wendell Holmes, Jr. would have started from the premise that legislatures as much as courts are the ultimate guardians of our liberties. But then he would have gone on to distinguish between review of state and federal legislative acts.

As he once said: "I do not think the United States would come to an end if we had no power to declare an act of Congress void. I do think that the Union would be imperiled if we could not make that declaration as to the laws of the several states."

In light of that statement, chances are good that Holmes would not have voted with Marshall in *Marbury.*

Louis Brandeis's attitude toward judicial review is most clearly seen in his concurring opinion in *Ashwander* v. *TVA.* There he listed several rules to avoid passing on the constitutionality of an act of Congress, noting, "The most important thing we do is not doing." Brandeis might well have used one of those rules to avoid a constitutional clash in *Marbury.*

For example, Brandeis could easily and fairly have construed the statute in question so as to avoid a conflict with the Constitution. He might well have argued, with genuine merit, that the statute's reference to "writs of mandamus" was meant to be part of the Supreme Court's appellate jurisdiction. After all, the reference occurs in a sentence discussing appellate jurisdiction, and the language, structure, and purpose of the sentence point in the same direction.

Finding no conflict between the original jurisdiction given the Court by the Constitution and the appellate jurisdiction granted by the statute, Brandeis perhaps would have avoided worrying about the Court's power to nullify an act of Congress.

Owen Roberts belongs in this august company solely because of his famous statement: "When an act of Congress is appropriately challenged in the courts as not conforming to the constitutional mandate the judicial branch has only one duty,—to lay the article of the Constitution which is invoked beside the statute which is challenged and to decide whether the latter squares with the former."

Perhaps Roberts would have perceived no conflict because the statute was a contemporaneous construction of the Constitution. Congress passed the Judiciary Act of 1789 only two years after the Constitution itself was drafted. The Congress that wrote the statute contained many men who participated in the drafting of the Constitution. Presumably they knew what they intended the constitutional grant of original jurisdiction to mean. Their contemporaneous construction is entitled to respect.

Felix Frankfurter is another easy subject. His oft-expressed views on judicial restraint, in which he opposed interference with co-equal branches of government, make it at least a strong possibility that he would have shied away from judicial review in *Marbury*. The case might well have struck Frankfurter as nonjusticiable because it posed a "political question." Public confidence in the Court's moral sanctions, he once wrote, "must be nourished by the Court's complete detachment, in fact and in appearance, from political entanglements and by abstention from injecting itself into the clash of political forces in political settlements."

Elsewhere he said, "We need to frankly acknowledge that there is not under our Constitution a judicial remedy for every political mischief, for every undesirable exercise of legislative power. The Framers carefully and with deliberate forethought refused so to enthrone the judiciary." It is not hard to imagine Marshall and Frankfurter disagreeing on the proper judicial approach to *Marbury* v. *Madison*.

Hugo Black might have taken a more subtle approach. While he might have agreed that the Court has constitutional power to strike down statutes, state or federal, that violate specific commands of the federal Constitution, Black could have concluded that no such specific constitutional command was at issue in *Marbury*. After all, nothing in the Constitution says its grant of original jurisdiction to the Court is exclusive.

If his dissent in *Griswold* v. *Connecticut* is any guide, Black could easily distinguish the issues in *Marbury* from cases involving violations of the specific provisions of the Bill of Rights. The Constitution does not say: "Congress shall make no law granting to the Supreme Court original jurisdiction in cases other than those here specified." Congress, Black might have concluded, has a right to act unless prohibited by some specific constitutional provision.

Our imaginary survey shows a vote of seven (Field, Sutherland, Brandeis, Holmes, Roberts, Frankfurter and Black) to two (Marshall and Taney) against the position actually taken by the Court in 1803. But part of Marshall's greatness, as Holmes once pointed out, consists in his being at "a strategic point in the campaign of history."

Of course, there is no way to test the accuracy of our surprising little canvass, and it is, to be sure, shot through with speculation and omissions of scores of justices. Still, it is enlightening and stimulating to wonder what might have happened if *Marbury* had gone the other way, and further, how many other basic legal principles are open to the same conjecture.

5

Legal Fundamentalism

THERE is a new and serious threat to law as we now know it—the threat of religious fundamentalism. This threat could change our most basic concepts of law, legal philosophy, and the judicial process. Religious fundamentalism as applied to law—call it Legal Fundamentalism—demands our attention, lest we be caught unawares as it alters the foundations of our legal system.

Religious fundamentalism is based on moral absolutism derived from religious sources. Reacting to what they see as morals that are man-made, subjective, and without solid foundation, conservative evangelicals espouse moral positions believed to be grounded in divine authority. Evangelicals view these morals as immutable. Those who fail to heed these morals—who "ignore the guidance of God"—are sinners motivated by Satan. Religious fundamentalism is marked by an authoritarian, literalist, and doctrinaire attitude.

The most obvious manifestations of Legal Fundamentalism are growing efforts to change specific laws. Congress is considering, more seriously than ever, a constitutional amendment to allow religious prayers in public schools. Creationists are starting lawsuits reminiscent of the *Scopes* monkey trial to require textbooks to include religious theories side-by-side with scientific theories about the origin of the universe and evolution. Those who want to overrule the Supreme Court's 1973 abortion decisions get louder and louder with each passing year.

A more subtle and virulent danger of Legal Fundamentalism is its intolerant cast, tone, and style. If God is on your side, then anyone who disagrees with you is godless and an agent of Satan. You are right and he is wrong. The trouble is that each of us thinks *he* is right. Intolerant Legal Fundamentalism, if it becomes the dominant mode of legal thinking, would inevitably chill dissent in thought and behavior, and threaten pluralism, intellectual freedom, and democracy itself.

Worst of all, Legal Fundamentalism will affect our habits of legal thought, our attitudes toward law. It could transform legal thinking. Sad to say, the transformation will be reactionary and take us back to an earlier and rejected era in legal thinking.

The characteristics of Legal Fundamentalism are well known. Legal Fundamentalism sees man-made rules as too subjective and unsound. Under Legal Fundamentalism, law will cease making claims on the Constitution, statutes, precedents and policy considerations. Law will invoke, rather, a higher authority. It will rely on a type of revelation.

In many respects, Legal Fundamentalism closely resembles Legal Formalism, that discredited jurisprudential doctrine that dominated America between the Civil War and early in this century. Under Legal Formalism, judges did not "make" law; they "discovered" it. The law was thought to be immutable and affected with almost supernatural quality. It was as if judges were regarded as high priests of the law, which they "announced" as revealed to them.

The devastating criticisms of Legal Formalism by Holmes, Cardozo & Co. apply with equal force to Legal Fundamentalism. The alleged divine authority would mask the true human source of law. Though men might deny it, they would still "make" the law. Interpretation, avowed or not, would continue. Without interpretation and adaptation, law would ossify and be unacceptable. Legal Fundamentalism, like Legal Formalism, is a gigantic fraud that feeds on man's gullibility.

Legal Fundamentalism contrasts sharply with our current notions of law. Today, we think of law as based on empirical experience, as a pragmatic device for accomplishing specific political, economic, and social objectives. Law is made by human beings to satisfy the needs of human beings. It starts from the premise that, in Learned Hand's phrase, it is "not sure it is right," and therefore fosters tolerance in a pluralist society. As the New York Court of Appeals said in 1980, "It is not the function of the Penal Law in our governmental polity to provide either a medium for the articulation or the apparatus for the intended enforcement of moral or theological values."

In general, law today tries to derive sound ethical standards from human reason based on experience, not disembodied logic or divine authority. We insist that judges lay bare their reasons for deciding a particular way. It is not enough simply to render a decision without explanation. We discuss judicial opinions in terms of policy considerations. We permit judges to dissent, which rather undercuts the notion of one true legal interpretation. We recognize the law changes over time and often with the political winds.

Modern law and Legal Fundamentalism, Reason and Faith—these seem to be opposite poles. Indeed the Winter

1980 issue of the *Mercer Law Review,* devoted to a symposium on "The Secularization of Law," contains an extraordinary collection of articles generally bemoaning the radical separation of law and religion in twentieth century American thought in the sphere of jurisprudence and legal philosophy. Reading these curious articles makes one feel uneasy, as if the last hundred years of legal history had never occurred. What can one say, for example, when a distinguished Harvard law professor (Harold Berman) criticizes law "measured only by standards of experience, of workability, and not by standards of truth and rightness"? Whose "truth"? Whose "rightness"? The law school that bred such champions of tolerance as Holmes and Brandeis should blush.

According to Legal Fundamentalism, the present sorry state of the law began with the Enlightenment in the eighteenth century. Before the Age of Reason, law supposedly was something ordained, something at least partly given. Following the Enlightenment, law was seen as something wholly instrumental, wholly invented. But, in the words of Professor Berman, "Prior to World War I, and even up to the Great Depression, Americans, as a people, continued to believe that the Constitution and the legal system were rooted in a covenant made with God." The Enlightenment concept of law as man-made has penetrated our ideology "only within the last two generations."

But Legal Fundamentalism somehow misses the crucial point of the historical analysis. The period before the first third of the twentieth century, when Americans believed in a religious theory of law, corresponds to our heyday of Legal Formalism. Our modern theory of law, flowering "only within the last two generations," replaced Legal Formalism. To fail even to mention Legal Formalism in this context is to ignore the obvious. The most cursory glance at history thus shows the true nature of Legal Fundamentalism: a yearning for the bygone era of Legal Formalism.

But exposing Legal Fundamentalism for what it truly is, is only the beginning. In *The Heavenly City of the Eighteenth Century Philosophers*, historian Carl Becker argued that the Enlightenment dethroned organized religion and in its place deified reason. Are we the new *philosophes*? Have we deluded ourselves into thinking that by rejecting Legal Formalism or Legal Fundamentalism we do anything more than substitute one form of religion for another? We must be careful not to make law itself into our civil religion. As Americans start lawsuits to vindicate more and more rights, to challenge governmental action, to promote social change, the worship of law itself seems to become a religion and a faith. We should be wary of raising altars to a beautiful Goddess of Law.

It appears to be much a matter of cycles. Throughout history, the forces of mysticism have warred with the Life of Reason. Men wearied with life, and harrassed with war, social and economic troubles and turmoil, and with general uncertainty, have periodically flocked back to faith, and covered their retreat with an appeal to instinct and feeling. Today the battle must be fought anew; the ways of reason embodied in our modern concept of law must be defended once more against instinct, intuition, mysticism, and unintelligible and intolerant faith.

In short, Legal Fundamentalism makes us face again the central problem that harassed Socrates: if supernatural sanctions have ceased to influence the behavior of men, how shall we find another ethic to replace them? Unfortunately, Legal Fundamentalism supplies the wrong answer.

6

The Ages of American Law

"THE worse the society, the more law there will be. In Hell there will be nothing but law, and due process will be meticulously observed." With this seemingly contradictory but perceptive comment, Professor Grant Gilmore winds up *The Ages of American Law,* the expanded book version of his 1974 Storr Lectures at Yale.

Gilmore is either overly modest or overly cute when he disclaims making a contribution to the scholarly literature, unless intellectual fare is measured nowadays solely by the number and size of footnotes and other conventional documentation. For the truth is that Gilmore offers us, in readily digestible form, the benefits of a lifetime of legal scholarship, with an insight here, a hypothesis there, and balanced judgment throughout.

Gilmore's thesis is that three basic and distinct periods mark the history of American law. The first period, dubbed the Age of Discovery by Gilmore, lasted from 1800 to the Civil War, and was the Golden Age of American law. Those were the days when American lawyers and judges had the chance and the duty to make a fresh start, to fashion a nation. Unlike contemporary English judges, who, in the wake of Blackstone, were by and large stressing adherence to precedent, American judges in the early 1800s showed a lighthearted disregard for precedent and a joyous acceptance of the idea that they were supposed to make law. Gilmore likens this frontier attitude to the approach taken by the great Lord Mansfield in England fifty or seventy-five years earlier, and points out that the problems facing our industrialized society in the 1820s resembled those with which English courts dealt during the heyday of Mansfieldianism.

The Age of Discovery did not see a successful codification movement. But the idea of national uniformity did take on significance throughout the specifically American contribution of authoritative learned treatises. Although Gilmore dismisses the success of Kent's *Commentaries* as "unmerited," he praises Joseph Story's many treatises for their scholarship and originality. "Nothing like them, in English, had ever been seen before," according to Gilmore. "For the better part of a hundred years no books of comparable excellence were produced in any English-speaking country."

Gilmore uses the Supreme Court's ill-starred decision in *Swift* v. *Tyson* to illustrate the Grand Style of the Age of Discovery. Dealing first with the substance of *Swift* v. *Tyson*, Gilmore shows that by ignoring an obvious solution to a simple case, the Court decided to "use the ridiculous case as the opportunity for federalizing—or nationalizing—a large part of the common law of the United States." Then Gilmore moves on to a less obvious but perhaps more important aspect of the case: the process of adjudication which Story's opinion favored. Story counseled in favor of a policy-oriented approach to law, one that did not take a narrow view of precedent, looked to *all* the available literature, and considered social and economic consequences. Gilmore calls *Swift* v. *Tyson* "one of the most eloquent, as it was one of the most influential statements" of the creative and innovative spirit that characterized American law during the pre-Civil War period.

By contrast with the Age of Discovery, the Age of Faith—running from the Civil War to World War I—was a dispiriting period of unrelieved formalism. It assumed that law is a closed, logical system. During the Age of Faith, judges did not make law: they merely discovered and declared what the true rules of law were and indeed always had been. Truth being immutable and eternal, there was no adaptation of rules of law to changing conditions. This was the age of the string citation; the facts and reasons behind past decisions remained unexplored.

According to Gilmore, the twin symbols of the Age of Faith are Christopher Columbus Langdell and Oliver Wendell Holmes, Jr. Langdell, the first dean of the Harvard Law School in 1870, is described as "an essentially stupid man who, early in his life, hit on one great idea to which, thereafter, he clung with all the tenacity of genius." (Langdell would have struck Isaiah Berlin as a hedgehog rather than a fox.) The idea of Langdell and his followers was that law is a science and that theories could be formulated to cover broad areas of the common law and reduce everything to as few hypotheses as possible, preferably one. Progressive simplification—a legal version of Occam's Razor—became the prevailing jurisprudential approach.

Everyone, including Holmes, searched for a unitary set of rules to cover all possible situations. Whereas Langdell's thought was "crude and simplistic," and Holmes's thought was "subtle and sophisticated," Holmes too spent his time trying to fit cases in a "philosophically continuous series" and construct a unitary theory.

The contributions of Langdell and Holmes may have been dwarfed, in Gilmore's estimation, by the West Publishing Company's establishment of the National Reporter System during the 1880s. Decisions of the highest state courts, as well as those from federal appellate courts, became available and, being available, had to be used.

After the Age of Faith came the Age of Anxiety, from World War I to the recent past. Symbolized by Cardozo, Corbin, and so-called Legal Realists, the Age of Anxiety led to the disintegration of unitary theory and a return toward a pre-Langdellian pluralism. At the time it was heresy for Cardozo to confess in *The Nature of the Judicial Process* that judges occasionally made law instead of merely declaring it. Facts not theory became key during this period.

Gilmore's tripartite division makes sense and serves well as the backdrop for an exciting and lively little intellectual history of American law. Blessed with a clean and lean style, Gilmore condenses the sweep of centuries, putting movements and individual heros into perspective. Gilmore paints with a broad brush, and, as in his prior book *The Death of Contract*, takes a highly original and essentially philosophical approach to his subject.

7

Raising the Titanic

THE reports of the death of economic substantive due process may have been, in Mark Twain's famous phrase, greatly exaggerated. The funeral rites, embodied in cases and commentaries over the past forty years, now look a bit premature.

The rise and fall of judicial review of economic and social regulation is an oft-told tale. Around 1890, the Supreme Court began to void legislation in the economic and social realm on the asserted ground that such laws violated the Due-Process Clause of the Fourteenth Amendment by unlawfully depriving corporations of their liberty or property rights. For decades the Court would not only assess the means the legislature chose to achieve its objectives, but also its goals. This was the heyday of substantive due process, typified by cases like *Allgeyer* v. *Louisiana*, *Lochner* v. *New York*, and *Coppage* v. *Kansas*.

Not until the 1930s, under the lash of the Depression, did economic substantive due process seem to pass away. That doctrine was savagely criticized for permitting judges to void legislation simply because they thought the legislation unwise. The economic dislocation of the Depression finally drove home the need for affirmative action by government. Courts, accordingly, developed a new test, one more respectful of the positive role of legislation in the achievement of social and economic goals. This new test—the rational basis test—upheld the constitutionality of a statute so long as it was neither arbitrary nor irrational.

The legal metamorphosis from substantive due process to rational basis in the economic sphere appeared complete. In the past few decades, the Supreme Court has treated challenges to economic regulation with a broad "hands-off" approach. No such statute has been invalidated on substantive due process grounds since 1937. By 1963, the Supreme Court was able to stress "our abandonment of the use of the 'vague contours' of the Due Process Clause to nullify laws which a majority of the Court believed unwise . . . Whether the legislature takes for its textbook Adam Smith, Herbert Spencer, Lord Keynes, or some other is no concern of ours." Economic substantive due process surely seemed, as legal doctrine, to be dead and to have received a decent burial.

But now there is mounting proof of a resurrection.

One significant item of evidence is a recent concurring opinion by Judge Jacob Fuchsberg of the New York Court of Appeals. In *Town of North Hempstead* v. *Exxon Corporation*, decided in May 1981, that court rejected a classical due process challenge to a local law prohibiting self-service gasoline station pumps, finding that the legislative judgment was not irrational. Although Judge Fuchsberg agreed with the court's brief memorandum opinion, he took the occasion to discuss the controlling "pattern of principles" for evaluating a due process attack on the constitutionality of legislation in the economic sphere, principles, according to Judge Fuchsberg, "never articulated in perspective."

Fuchsberg's concurrence amounted to an invitation to state courts to use a new version of economic substantive due process. In the very first paragraph of his opinion, he noted that, "to fill this gap [created by the Supreme Court's hands-off approach] in an age when governmental legislative and quasi-legislative intervention in economic affairs abounds, courts in most states, relying on their own constitutions, have reasserted a right, albeit somewhat limited, to scrutinize and, where appropriate, invalidate offending regulation." Later on, after describing the rational basis test, Fuchsberg said: "This judicial deference to the legislative judgment has not been without its critics, who have deplored what they took to be an overreaction substituting a well-nigh 'all-out tolerance' of economic regulation for the 'inflexible negativism' characterizing the days of *Lochner*." And just in case anyone missed the message, Fuchsberg repeated what he said at the outset, that "most of our state courts, applying their own constitutional provisions on the order of due process and equal protection, have not hesitated to reassert a right to thereby scrutinize and, where appropriate, invalidate economic legislation."

Judge Fuchsberg's concurring opinion in *Exxon* came down at about the same time a related book came out. In *Economic Liberties and the Constitution*, published by the University of Chicago Press, Bernard H. Seigin argues that the Supreme Court is responsible for the allegedly excessive economic regulation in our society. Referring to the demise of economic substantive due process and the rise of the rational basis test, the author points out that since the 1940s, the Court has done nothing about laws that limit the right of individuals or private corporations to engage in legitimate economic activities. The result, according to Seigin, has been to give governments at all levels much greater power over the economic system and to harm society by inhibiting production, raising prices, curtailing competition, and creating unemployment.

The practically simultaneous publication of Fuchsberg's striking concurrence and Seigin's new book strongly suggests the start of a trend. Now in its incipiency, that trend may well grow in tandem with the mood of the nation under the influence of President Reagan's limited approach to governmental regulation. Indeed, an advertisement for Seigin's book carries a warm endorsement from presidential advisor Edwin Meese. We should therefore not be overly surprised by more doctrinal development along the lines suggested by Fuchsberg and Seigin.

Given these realities, we should at least try to grasp the implications of what is happening.

First of all, we should not necessarily be dismayed. In burying economic substantive due process, the Supreme Court may have gone too far. The re-emerging doctrine may have new elements born of past legal and economic experience and without the social and economic animus that prevailed around 1900. If neo-substantive due process can erect meaningful objective standards apart from personal value systems, if it can refine ways for better testing the rationality of legislative action, then perhaps we will all gain. The new doctrine, in reality, may represent a more mature approach to a genuine problem.

The new doctrine should also prompt welcome reexamination of the preferred-position theory. Under that theory, courts now scrutinize much more carefully laws in the civil liberties area. When the first edition of economic substantive due process came out, it was the reverse, with civil liberties getting less attention than economic liberties. Is the current distinction between "economic" and "civil liberties" cases sufficiently clear to justify the differences in judicial scrutiny? Is the "liberty" of the individual who is denied a master electrician's license under a guild-type state law all that different from the kind of "liberty" protection in free speech and race discrimination cases? Is there any constitutional or philosophical justification for the present degree of difference in the judicial attitudes toward the two types of legislation?

From another viewpoint, the new doctrine highlights and strengthens what the Supreme Court has called "our federalism." Just because the Supreme Court reads the United States Constitution in a certain way does not mean state courts must necessarily read their state constitutions the same way. Criminal defense attorneys have argued with some success that Supreme Court interpretations of federal constitutional law are no bar to state courts reading their analogous state constitutional safeguards so as to provide defendants with protections not afforded by the Supreme Court. By the same token, due-process and equal-protection provisions in state constitutions may call for stricter scrutiny of economic and social regulation than the Supreme Court is prepared to read into their federal counterparts. Of course, practitioners must be alert to base their claims on state as well as federal constitutional law.

Finally, the new version of economic substantive due process should make us more sensitive to the nature of law. For more than a generation, economic substantive due process was so ridiculed and so discredited that few took it seriously. Now, with a longer perspective, we may be able to see that important legal doctrines usually reflect some deep and legitimate concerns (although the doctrine may become warped or counterproductive), and that while the particular doctrine may lose popularity, the concerns that gave rise to the doctrine do not completely go away. If the concern arises again, from political, economic, or social change, or for whatever reason, so may the need for the doctrine that had become unfashionable. Hopefully, the drawbacks of the old doctrine will be eliminated, and the new doctrine tempered by the wisdom of experience.

Still, the prospect of taking economic substantive due process out of the dustbins of constitutional theory strikes a young lawyer weaned on recent Supreme Court decisions as about as likely as raising the *Titanic*.

8

Ayn Rand's Legal World

IN AN important and much-publicized speech in October 1980, U.S. Attorney General William French Smith condemned "subjective judicial policy-making." It is a condemnation frequently made by many critics of court decisions. Subjectivism is, for such critics, the root cause of judicial transgressions. Presumably the critics favor the opposite of subjectivism, which is objectivism.

Objectivism calls to mind the philosophy of writer Ayn Rand. For years she published "The Objectivist Newsletter" and taught her disciples what she meant by objectivism. But the heart of Ayn Rand's appeal has always been her fiction. Perhaps we can glimpse the ideal legal world of critics of subjectivism by looking at the legal world that exists in the fiction of Ayn Rand.

Ayn Rand's fiction is powerful stuff. Her two big novels, *The Fountainhead* and *Atlas Shrugged*, have stirred millions of readers. In both books, the protagonists are highly gifted and able individuals who must struggle against society to realize, in spectacular ways, their creativity and success. This conflict between the individual and the collective, with the individual ultimately winning, is the basic theme of each novel.

It would belabor the obvious to note the similarity between the rugged individualism and laissez-faire economics of Ayn Rand's novels and the social and economic philosophy of the Reagan Administration. What is less obvious but perhaps more interesting is to draw out from Ayn Rand's work her views about law and lawyers.

Ayn Rand would probably agree with the critique of "subjective judicial policy-making." "Humanity's darkest evil, the most destructive horror machine among all the devices of men," says one of Ayn Rand's fictional characters, "is non-objective law." It is hard to tell the difference between what Ayn Rand calls "nonobjective law" and what critics call "subjective judicial policy-making." They are only slightly different ways of saying the same thing.

Ayn Rand frequently talks of the need for law that is objective. "Men need an institution charged with the task of protecting their rights under an *objective* code of rules. *This* is the task of government—of a *proper* government— its basic task, its only moral justification and the reason why men do need a government. *A government is the means of placing the retaliatory use of physical force under objective control*—i.e., under objectively defined laws." "All laws must be objective (and objectively justifiable)." "A complex legal system, based on objectively valid principles, is required to make a society free and *to keep it free.*"

The highly abstract nature of such remarks makes it somewhat difficult to know precisely what "objective law" means. It is also difficult to know how legal objectivism relates to legal philosophy. Is legal objectivism another term for Legal Formalism, by which judges feigned objectivity? More concrete meaning may emerge from the clash between society and the individual as depicted by Ayn Rand.

To dramatize the clash between the individual and society, Ayn Rand often uses the device of a trial. In both *The Fountainhead* and *Atlas Shrugged*, a courtroom trial of a hero takes place. In *The Fountainhead*, architect Howard Roark, whose buildings challenged a tradition-bound profession, faces criminal charges for dynamiting a housing project because his original design was changed. The trial is the book's highpoint.

Roark has no lawyer; he represents himself. He picks his own jury, choosing jurors with the hardest faces. "A lawyer would have chosen the gentlest types," writes Rand, "those most likely to respond to an appeal for mercy." The prosecutor opens to the jury by describing Roark as "a builder who became a destroyer," and then calls his witnesses, who testify for the prosecution without cross-examination by defendant Roark. After the prosecution rests, Roark announces: "Your honor, I shall call no witnesses. This will be my testimony and summation."

Roark's courtroom speech is unforgettable. The following passages capture the essence: "Throughout the centuries there were men who took first steps down new roads armed with nothing but their own vision. Their goals differed, but they all had this in common: that the step was first, the road new, the vision unborrowed, and the response they received—hatred. The great creators—the thinkers, the artists, the scientists, the inventors—stood alone against the men of their time . . . The degree of a man's independence, initiative and personal love for his work determines his talent as a worker and his worth as a man." After Roark's speech, the hard-faced jury took no time at all to return a verdict of not guilty.

There is a similar trial scene in *Atlas Shrugged*. There, Hank Rearden, a steel industrialist, is charged with breaking an economic regulation. Like Roark, Rearden goes to trial without a lawyer and wins over the courtroom with a plea on his own behalf, though he refuses to present any formal defense. After Rearden's speech, "The crowd burst into applause." The three judges imposed a suspended sentence, to more applause.

For another look at Ayn Rand's concept of law, we need only listen to one of the characters in *Atlas Shrugged,* retired Judge Narragansett, "one of those old-fashioned monks of the bench who thinks like a mathematician and never feels the human side of anything." "The law . . . ?" said Judge Narragansett, "What law? I did not give it up—it has ceased to exist. But I am still working in the profession I had chosen, which was that of serving the cause of justice . . . No, justice has not ceased to exist. How could it? It is possible for men to abandon their sight of it, and then it is justice that destroys them. But it is not possible for justice to go out of existence, because one is an attribute of the other, because justice is the act of acknowledging that which exists."

A little later, Judge Narragansett explains why he left the bench. "I quit when the court of appeals reversed my ruling. The purpose for which I had chosen my work, was my resolve to be a guardian of justice. But the laws they asked me to enforce made me the executor of the vilest injustice conceivable. I was asked to use force to violate the rights of disarmed men, who came before me to seek my protection for their rights. Litigants obey the verdict of a tribunal solely on the premise that there is an *objective* rule of conduct, which they both accept. Now I saw that justice was to consist of upholding the unjustifiable. I quit—because I could not have borne to hear the words 'Your Honor' addressed to me by an honest man." In fiction, at least, judges resign for reasons other than money.

Ayn Rand also connects law and individual liberties. "'Rights' are a moral concept," she says, "the link between the moral code of a man and the legal code of a society, between ethics and politics. Individual rights are the means of subordinating society to moral law." "The purpose of law and of government is the protection of individual rights." But it is precisely in this area of individual rights that Ayn Rand makes even ardent admirers pause.

Individual rights depend on tolerance, a quality Ayn Rand lacks. "A basic premise is an absolute that permits no cooperation with its antithesis and tolerates no tolerance." That kind of rigid statement is inconsistent with pluralism. It hardly encourages dissent from the party line. If there is one basic flaw in Ayn Rand's legal philosophy, it is this contradiction between concern for individual rights and the clear tone of intolerant dogmatism. Even with this flaw, however, Ayn Rand's legal world has something to teach us lawyers. A lawyer need not agree with all of Ayn Rand's legal philosophy to be moved by her character portrayal. Ayn Rand's characters inspire. The first time I stayed up all night to write a brief, I imagined I was Howard Roark working all night on a set of drawings for his mentor Henry Cameron. Whenever I feel like doing something easier than practicing law, I think of Dagny Taggart (the heroine of *Atlas Shrugged*) and her refusal to join the strike of the men of the mind. And when I left a Park Avenue law firm to be a single practitioner and then to form a new law firm, I hoped that Roark, Hank Rearden, Dagny, and Francisco would have smiled approvingly and said, "Well done."

Ideals bring out the best within us; they make life worth living.

9

Pro Bono Magnifico

IN FEBRUARY 1972 a coal company's huge coalwaste refuse pile, which dammed a stream in the West Virginia mountains, collapsed without warning and sent water and sludge rampaging through Buffalo Creek Valley below. Over 125 people, mostly miners' wives and children, died at once and the thousand homes in Buffalo Creek Valley were destroyed. A few hundred of the survivors banded together to sue the coal company. The story of the survivors' lawsuit was told, in *The Buffalo Creek Disaster*, by the lawyer who represented them.

At the time of the Buffalo Creek disaster, Gerald M. Stern was a young litigation partner at the Washington law firm of Arnold & Porter. Before joining the firm he was a trial attorney with the Civil Rights Division of the U.S. Justice Department, trying voting-discrimination cases. In 1969, Arnold & Porter started a commendable program of permitting one partner each year to spend all of his time on *pro bono* cases. Stern was in the middle of his stint as Arnold & Porter's *pro bono* partner when the killer flood hit unsuspecting Buffalo Creek. Until then, Stern's *pro bono* year had left him restless, he "hadn't found any case to fill my days and nights, to make me feel bigger than myself."

The Buffalo Creek disaster ended Stern's restlessness.

Retained on a contingent basis, Arnold & Porter lawyers led by Stern started by interviewing potential plaintiffs. Those interviews, filled as they are with vivid memories of genuine tragedies, form the most moving portion of Stern's account. One miner, for instance, told how he, his wife and two-year-old son were separated as they were swept along by the flood; how the wife's last words were "take care of my baby," and how the baby in the miner's arms died from swallowing too much water.

Once the survivors' stories were heard, the next task for Stern was to draft a complaint. Inasmuch as the plaintiffs were survivors, Stern decided that the main thrust of the complaint should be for psychic impairment caused by the flood, which in turn resulted from the coal company's gross negligence and reckless conduct in constructing and maintaining the dam. The theory, known to psychologists and psychiatrists as survival syndrome, was that the survivors, whether or not actually touched by the flood waters, suffered great guilt from having lost homes, neighborhoods, and loved ones. The complaint, after amendment, was brought as a diversity suit in federal court on behalf of 625 plaintiffs and sought $64 million in damages. The defendant was the local coal company's out-of-state parent.

The history of the Buffalo Creek lawsuit is a tribute to the value of thorough preparation. Stern's effective use of pretrial discovery, as well as his apparent willingness to go to trial, broke the defendant's nerve and led to a whopping $13.5 million settlement, $3 million of which was Arnold & Porter's contingent fee. (Arnold & Porter obviously derived real, as well as psychic, income from this *pro bono* venture.) As Stern puts it, "Sometimes that is all you do in the law. You just keep pressing ahead until the other side cracks."

Stern's book is really two books, one about Buffalo

Creek, the other about the litigating process. Besides the lucid and crisp narrative of the Buffalo Creek suit, the book contains throughout many interesting and suggestive comments about the nature of litigators and litigation.

What true litigator, for example, does not long for a case that will "become [my] life, filling all [my] waking hours with excitement and purpose"? What litigator negotiating a settlement on the eve of trial has not, like Stern, "wonder[ed] whether a good settlement also should include some payment to me for giving up the right to try the case"?

While discussing depositions in the case, Stern describes some of the qualifications of a cross-examiner: "I like to cross-examine, to get into someone else's mind, to find out what he really knows or thinks. I don't like not knowing, and I'm not very trusting. I'm also willing to ask questions, and I don't mind, too much, appearing ignorant, asking the obvious, going over a simple answer again."

More than once, Stern betrays a distaste for dry and confusing legal prose. Of a more definite statement he prepared in the case, Stern says: "It was not a typical legal document. It spoke to the heart, not the brain." About a preliminary procedural skirmish: "It is true that lawyers' arguments never seem to get to the point. But sometimes that is the point."

"Lawyers," writes Stern, "object to one-word sentences." Whether that generalization is true or not, Stern's book can be fittingly described in a one-word sentence. Superb.

10

The Morality of Contract

REEXAMINING a major premise is always in order. Most logical errors are embedded in a major premise uncritically accepted. And so it is with the law of contracts.

A major premise of contract law, at least since Holmes's lectures on *The Common Law*, has been its lack of a moral component. Holmes thought law in general moved from subjective fault toward a point where the subjective mind of the defendant is irrelevant. According to Holmes, everyone "is free to break his contract if he chooses," with the only result being a duty to pay compensatory damages. (Holmes forgot about specific performance.) Inasmuch as a breach of contract is neither moral nor immoral, no punitive damages flow from a breach. In the Holmesian theory, contract had, in short, no basis in morals.

This premise comes under strict scrutiny in a book by Harvard law professor Charles Fried. In *Contract as Promise: A Theory of Contractual Obligation*, Fried argues powerfully for a moral basis of contract law. His book sails manfully against the current.

Fried digs away in the foundations of some of our deepest assumptions about contract. He reopens painful questions about turnings taken in the course of the development of contract theory. Fried calls into question some of the most deeply held assumptions of contract law. He tries to analyze and lay bare the origins and nature of the often implicit, deeply embedded, formative ideas surrounding contract law.

The key to Fried's moral theory of contract is what Fried calls the "promise principle," the principle by which persons bind themselves because they choose to do so. The promise principle, with its stress on contractual obligation as being essentially self-imposed, derives from liberal individualism and autonomy. "The regime of contract law . . . carries to its natural conclusion the liberal premise that individuals have rights."

A promise engenders trust in the promisee, and thereby involves morality. The promisor creates expectations in others, and it is wrong, according to Fried drawing on Kant's categorical imperative, not to fulfill such expectations. "By promising, we transform a choice that was morally neutral into one that is morally compelled."

Is promise, with its overtones of morality, *the* central principle of contract theory? Some writers think the search for a unifying principle is a will-o'-the-wisp. Even Fried claims less than universal and comprehensive scope for the promise principle. The challenge for him is to show that the promise principle can hold its own against rival moral principles, while leaving them room to effect such substantial justice as lies within their particular domains.

Within the domain of the promise principle, expectation interest is the measure of what a promise is worth. Expectation interest represents, in the old and tired phrase, benefit of the bargain. Of course, there are situations where the "expectation" measure is inappropriate, but those exceptions in no way gut Fried's theory.

Where the promise principle and the expectation measure somehow fail to work, Fried looks to two competing residuary principles of civil obligation. The first of these is the "benefit principle," which encompasses the concepts of unjust enrichment and restitution and is designed to compensate for benefits conferred. The second is the "reliance principle," which focuses on the injury suffered by plaintiff as a result of relying on a promise and asks if defendant is responsible.

In compensating for harm done, the reliance principle is, as Fried points out, a special case of tort liability. It signifies an attempt to assimilate contracts to tort. By doing so, it subordinates the individualistic promise principle to collective standards and ends.

These residuary principles play a large role in defending Fried's model from attack. Critics of the promise principle often point to cases involving mistake, frustration, and impossibility as glaring examples of the inadequacy of promise as a means of explaining contract law. Fried's answer is beautifully simple. All such cases, according to Fried, involve kinds of surprises. Although the parties seem to have agreed, and even think they have agreed, actually they have not agreed about an important aspect of the transaction. The contract has a gap.

In filling the contractual gaps, courts must therefore use principles external to the parties' will. "When relations between parties are not governed by the actual promises they have made, they are governed by residual general principles of law." We are all familiar with judicial efforts to find the presumed intent of the parties or to adopt an objective theory of interpretation. To these, Fried adds the tort principle and the restitution principle, as well as another, perhaps more intriguing, principle.

Fried favors adopting what he calls the "sharing principle." The sharing principle would come into play where no agreement exists, no one in the relationship is at fault, and no one has conferred a benefit. It fills the theoretical void not occupied by the principles of promise, tort or restitution. At the same time, it softens the rigor and unfairness of leaving the loss where it lies. The sharing principle works by apportioning an unexpected loss among the parties according to fairness and equity. It represents a new and original contribution to contract theory, with important implications for the nature of the relationship between contracting parties.

Contractual relations, according to Fried, create a status and relationship with special duties and constraints. For this reason, the doctrine of good faith—which imposes obligations beyond the precise terms of the contract—is no real threat to the promise principle, that is, that promise is sufficient to define relations between contracting parties. Fried describes his position as a deliberate rejection and retreat from Henry Sumner Maine's classic thesis that progress is the movement "from Status to Contract."

But Fried and Maine are perfectly compatible. Maine says progress involves movement from Status to Contract. Fried says Contract creates a special status. The synthesis is that Status moves to Contract, which in turn creates a new Status. The crucial point is that the parties create their new status by virtue of their voluntary act of contracting. Fried's new, voluntary, freely chosen Status is a far cry from Maine's concept of Status as one's inherited, irrevocably frozen place in society.

The new status based on contract is an important concept, reflecting a development in the law that goes beyond contracts. As Jethro Lieberman points out in his recent book *The Litigious Society*, much of the changing face of the law in many areas is an attempt to charge a variety of relationships with a fiduciary character. Lieberman modifies Maine's famous dictum to say, "The course the law has taken may be denoted as a movement from *contract to fiduciary."* But Lieberman's formulation undercuts neither Maine nor Fried nor our synthesis of them both. After all, the parties are free to enter or not to enter the contract. Having exercised that free choice, they create obligations vis-à-vis each other. Contrary to what Lieberman says, society does not "constrain freedom of action by imposing a fiduciary duty"; it merely recognizes the consequences of such freedom of action.

One risk of Fried's approach is philosophical monism, the doctrine that all of contract law can be subsumed by one all-embracing theory. The danger is that, while the promise principle may afford novel and genuine insight, it may be too one-sided and over-simple, incapable of doing justice to the variety of possible fact patterns and relevant legal doctrines. But Fried avoids the danger of monism by noting the limits of the promise principle. "Nothing about the promise principle," concedes Fried, "entails that all disputes between people who have tried but failed to make a contract or who have broken a contract must be decided solely to that principle." He appropriately looks to residual legal principles to fill in gaps.

A perhaps more serious risk in Fried's theory is its quasi-fundamentalist tone. There is an absolutist cast to Fried's moralizing. At one point, for example, Fried writes: "The validity of a moral truth, like that of a mathematical truth, does not depend on fashion or favor." Elsewhere, he says morality "must be permanent and beyond our particular will." Aside from their uncharacteristically dogmatic style, such comments call to mind natural law theory, with all its flaws and subjectivity.

But such mild criticisms do not dilute Fried's achievements. His book is liberally laced with apt references to both classical and modern works of philosophy. Time and

again, Fried raises and illuminates, in light of vividly concrete hypotheticals, major issues with which he has dealt
in a more abstract manner in his philosophical passages.

All in all, Fried's book offers a sensitive and subtle investigation, a richly suggestive vision of contract theory. The
study and systematic critical discussion of such theory is of
the first importance, for it is a question of nothing less
than the relationship between law and morals.

11

Teaching, Scholarship, and Truth

NOT TOO long ago, an article in the Yale Law Journal accused practicing lawyers of two serious shortcomings. In a foreword to a symposium on legal scholarship, Yale law professor Anthony Kronman said, first, that teaching and scholarship "play little or no role in the life of the practicing lawyer." Second, he said that practicing attorneys are cynical, careless, and indifferent about the truth.

A double-barrelled accusation of such import deserves scrutiny.

To ignore the central role of teaching and scholarship in law practice is to misperceive what a practicing lawyer does. A new law school graduate is unprepared to try a case or draft a contract. Acquisition of lawyering skills is a long, cumulative process, heavily dependent on teaching by more experienced practitioners. Teaching by seasoned attorneys is how the profession passes on its standards and traditions.

Lawyers also teach their clients. Contact between lawyer and client is the most common point at which the public learns about the law. We teach by example—the advice we give, our attitudes, the way we comport ourselves. For the ordinary person, his or her lawyer symbolizes the law, in all its grandeur or all its pettiness.

Equally crucial to law practice is scholarship. Effective lawyering calls for a degree of scholarship on a par with the best in academia. Creativity and imagination, research and subtle analysis of precedent, discovery and application of implicit policy considerations behind legal rules, arguments for or against new rules, careful study of statutes and their history—all these and more are part of practicing law.

Scholarship in law practice is, moreover, scholarship with an edge. As Holmes once said: "It is one thing to utter a happy phrase from a protected cloister; another to think under fire—to think for action upon which great interests depend."

But scholarship differs from advocacy, according to Professor Kronman. "The defining characteristic of scholarship," he wrote, "is its preoccupation with the discovery of truth." Advocacy, in contrast, "is the construction of a convincing or persuasive argument." Kronman thought advocacy is concerned with truth "only as an aid to persuasion." From these observations, Kronman concluded that "the advocate is indifferent to truth," which makes the practicing attorney, in the professor's view, cynical and careless about truth.

Behind Kronman's conclusion is an unexamined premise about the meaning of truth. But unlike jesting Pilate, Kronman never asks, "What is truth?" Yet we need to ask the question to evaluate Kronman's definitions of advocacy (as indifference to truth) and of scholarship (as pursuit of truth).

What is truth in law? Of course it includes faithful rendition of facts, but beyond that it is less clear. Is there one true interpretation of the majestic but sometimes vague provisions of our Constitution? Is a judge-made rule a legal truth? If new legal rules supplant old ones, which are true?

Can we even talk of legal truth while we encourage dissenting opinions by judges?

Legal truth insofar as the term has meaning, is subtle and complex, a function of many factors, including value judgments and utility. "The juristic philosophy of the common law," wrote Cardozo, "is at bottom the philosophy of pragmatism. Its truth is relative, not absolute."

Truth is a sometime thing even in the most rigorous and exact of disciplines. What geometry held as true for 2,000 years had to be changed when faced with the disconcerting "truths" of non-Euclidean geometry. What physics held as true since Newton had to be reevaluated in light of relativity theory.

Lawyers, who have seen dissenting opinions become law, should mistrust those who say they have a monopoly on truth. Without cynicism and skepticism, moral absolutism finds fertile soil. When Truth with a capital T takes over, it may lead to punishing or eliminating those who disagree. The world has seen too many holy wars and religious and political persecutions not be wary of claims of Truth.

Yet much as the attorney-advocate wants to win, he or she is not indifferent to truth. Ethical rules, promulgated by attorney-advocates, require him or her, among other things, to disclose unfavorable precedents, to correct a client's fraud on the court, and to avoid the knowing use of false testimony. The whole adversary process assumes that truth will emerge, and to that end uses cross-examination, which Wigmore—a great legal scholar—called "the greatest legal engine ever developed for the discovery of truth."

Advocacy is no less important to a scholar than it is to a practicing lawyer. A lawyer advocates a position on behalf of a client; a scholar advocates a position on behalf of a point of view. There is, for example, little if any difference between what a lawyer does when he urges a particular reading of a constitutional or statutory provision and what a "scholar" does when he explicates, say, a literary text.

In assembling his findings and presenting his arguments, the scholar tries to persuade his audience of his point of view. He marshals his evidence as best he can, arranging it, stressing certain facts and explaining away others, all with an eye toward being a good advocate of his position.

Advocacy is a technique of argumentation, a tool, not an end. Anyone—lawyer or scholar—who deals in arguments must be an advocate, without reducing his or her passion for truth, while at the same time recognizing that truth has more than one dimension.

After all, any practicing lawyer knows at least this one truth: Just because you argue better doesn't mean you're right.

12

The Music of the Laws

WHEN we listen to good music, we do not usually think of law. On the contrary, we think about music, which is exactly as it should be. Yet music affects us in many ways. It calms, it excites, it angers and it saddens. Given the many different effects music has, it is perhaps excusable to ponder whether music can have an effect on us as lawyers.

The central link between music and law is interpretation. Both fields depend on textual interpretation. In music, scores provide the texts. In law, the texts are constitutions, statutes, ordinances, regulations, and cases. In each field, interpretation of texts is of immense importance.

The similarities between musical and legal interpretation come to light in the introduction to *Facing the Music*, a selection of articles by Harold C. Schonberg, former music critic for *The New York Times*. In it, Schonberg describes his personal reactions to various aspects of music. Although Schonberg writes nothing of law, what he says goes to the heart of what lawyers do.

Schonberg tells us, for instance, that "nobody can say much about a Beethoven symphony, but a great deal can be said about the interpretation and performance of the work. To make any cogent points about the interpretation of works of the past, however, a critic must know a great deal about the performing history of the work." We can say the same thing about sources of law.

"As a child," Schonberg "realized that performers 'did' things to music—sometimes elegantly and convincingly, sometimes outlandishly and stupidly. It puzzled me that pianists could play the same work so differently." As law students, we realized that judges and lawyers "did" things to precedents—sometimes elegantly and convincingly, sometimes outlandishly and stupidly. It probably still puzzles most of us that judges and lawyers can read the same precedents so differently.

Just as "each pianist had his own idea" of how the works "should go," so does each attorney.

In an eloquent passage that, with only slight alteration, could have been written about the legal process, Schonberg writes: "Thus anybody engaged in recreating the bare, mysterious notes and markings of a composer necessarily has to bring his own ideas to them. Notes alone mean nothing, except to the handful of people in the world who have the ability to read and translate into sounds in the inner ear a page of printed music. Notes have to be played, and it is the performer who has to be the intermediary between composer and listener. Music, then, is a reflection, an interpretation of the mind of the composer expressed through the mind of the performer."

Rewritten from the viewpoint of the law, the passage might read: Anyone engaged in applying the bare, mysterious words of a legislator or a judge necessarily has to bring his own ideas to them. Words alone mean nothing. Words have to be interpreted, and it is the lawyer or judge who has to be the intermediary between legislator and citizen. Law, then, is a reflection, an interpretation of the mind of the draftsman expressed through the mind of the lawyer or judge.

Schonberg goes on to say that he has "spent a good part of my life trying to figure out what 'authentic' performance is." Lawyers spend a good part of their lives trying to figure out what "authentic" interpretation is. In both fields, "It may be that the question is unanswerable, but," as Schonberg writes, "there are certain guidelines." In music, "There is in existence a continuity of performance tradition." In law, there is a similar continuity of interpretive tradition.

As lawyers, we know the tensions between interpretations based on "framers' intent" and "evolving standards." The same tensions plague music too. "Most musicians today insist that their primary aim is 'to express the wishes of the composer.' But every age sees a composer differently. In any case, the farther back we get, the less likely is it possible to express the wishes of the composer. Too many things have changed, not the least of which are the instruments themselves, not to mention pitch or problems of ornamentation." Indeed, in a book called *The Lives of the Great Composers*, Schonberg says, "Music is a continually evolving process."

Learned Hand once quipped that using a dictionary is the surest way to misread a statute. Schonberg, who probably has not read many of Judge Hand's opinions, has this to say: "The closer we try to 'express the message of the composer' by playing exactly what he wrote and no more, the farther we may be getting away from his message." Schonberg recounts how he harped on this point as a critic, "trying to break performers away from slavish literalism."

"Musicians," according to Schonberg, "at least are aware of the fact that something else besides a strict, literal reproduction of the notes is required." Presumably, lawyers and judges are aware of the same thing vis-à-vis words in legal texts.

The similarities between music and law are suggestive. They say something significant about the process of interpretation, something that goes beyond the boundaries of any particular discipline. There is, of course, no single orthodox interpretation of Mozart's Symphony in G Minor, any more than there is one authoritative reading of the Due Process Clause of the Fourteenth Amendment. Everything turns on the outlook of the interpreter, his background, his intellect, his hopes and his aspirations.

Music and law are both functions of their creators, and reflections of their minds and their reactions to the world in which they live. Just as we experience the world through the ears and mind of a Beethoven, Brahms, or Stravinsky when we hear their music, so we understand the world through the minds of the Framers, a particular legislature, or a judge, when we read their work product. We are in contact with minds and we must attempt identification with those minds. The closer the identification, the closer it is possible to come to an understanding of the creator's work.

For all we know, one night this week Zubin Mehta, who probably never even heard of *McCulloch* v. *Maryland*, will stand at his podium and whisper to the New York Philharmonic: "We must never forget that it is a *symphony* we are expounding."

13

Law and Hermeneutics

INTERPRETATION lies close to the heart of a lawyer's everyday task. Lawyers spend much of their professional lives interpreting. They interpret constitutions, statutes, cases, documents, and intentions of parties. They interpret the law for clients, for other lawyers, and for judges. Lawyers are, in a word, professional interpreters.

The study of interpretation is called *hermeneutics*. The word itself comes from an ancient Greek phrase for a broker's task of bringing together a buyer and a seller. The broker became, by way of analogy, an interpreter, whose job it is to mediate between text and reader. Hermeneutics as a discipline is as old as man's quest for meaning in words, signs, and symbols. Philosophers and theologians from ancient to modern times have practiced hermeneutics.

Although hermeneutics could aid almost any field of study, it is now most popular—indeed fashionable—as an academic form of literary criticism. Rare is the current volume of literary analysis that omits reference to hermeneutics. This literary use of hermeneutics is understandable. After all, the interpretation of literature is the interpretation of texts.

Inasmuch as interpretation, especially of texts, is so crucial to lawyers, hermeneutics should be of particular relevance to law. This relevance emerges rather clearly from even the most cursory look at the two chief schools of hermeneutics.

One school—the traditional "author-based theory"—focuses on the author's intended meaning. According to this school, the author's intention supplies the proper way to understand a text. By analyzing the text and evidence of the author's intent, author-based theory calls for an objective determination of an author's intended verbal meaning. That verbal meaning is changeless and determinate, and should be recognized as valid. For the author-based school, the aim of hermeneutics is simply to ascertain and clarify the verbal meaning of the author.

In sharp contrast, "reader-based" hermeneutics deals with the significance of a passage for us today. It concentrates on how the verbal meaning of the text becomes meaningful for different readers. One's perception of the work is considered part of the work itself. All interpretation, for reader-based theory, is guided by the interpreter's own viewpoint and preliminary understanding. The chief virtue of reader-based interpretation is said to be its power to keep the old texts alive and valuable, while its chief defect (according to critics) is its subjectivity and relativism.

These two chief schools of hermeneutics—author-based and reader-based—closely resemble two fundamental methods of legal analysis. Author-based hermeneutics makes the draftsmen's intent paramount. Reader-based theory focuses more on the "living-document" approach. When lawyers, judges, and professors disagree over the meaning of a particular text, they often divide into these two camps.

Take the death penalty, for example. The Eighth Amendment prohibits "cruel and unusual punishment." An author-based/framers'-intent approach looks to what the people who drafted that clause meant, specifically and in general. A reader-based/living-document approach examines the text in light of evolving standards. As the Supreme Court rulings on capital punishment show, lawyers instinctively utilize both approaches. The same can be said of countless other examples.

Despite the obvious relevance and utility of hermeneutics, the legal profession has yet to take full advantage of the science. The term itself is virtually unknown to lawyers. Lawyers proceed, as they have always done, making arguments as best they can to support one interpretation or another of a given text. But lawyers have never made a genuine or systematic effort to borrow and improve upon the techniques developed by those who have over the years refined hermeneutics in their fields. This is both sad and silly, for there is nothing wrong with adapting to law the skills and insights of another discipline.

The magnitude of the need for applying hermeneutics to law is nowhere better seen than in the most important debate now going on in constitutional law. As John Ely's book *Democracy and Distrust* shows, the current major battle pits "interpretivism" against "non-interpretivism." Interpretivism requires judges deciding constitutional issues to confine themselves to enforcing norms stated or clearly implied in the written Constitution. Non-interpretivism allows courts to go beyond that set of references and enforce norms not discoverable within the Constitution. Such a debate over fundamental issues, over "interpretation" really, would be clearly enhanced by use of hermeneutics.

Hermeneutics will undoubtedly be something less than a panacea. But that is all right. First we must see what hermeneutics has to offer; we must consider whether it can be sensibly transposed from literature to law. If it can, then we have an obligation to publicize the possibility of a coherent theory of interpretation, a new tool of immense power for lawyers.

A glimpse of this powerful new tool can be found in the first issue of the *Cardozo Law Review* (Spring 1979). There, in an article entitled "Law, Literature and Cardozo's Judicial Poetics," Prof. Richard H. Weisberg compares Cardozo to Flaubert and analyzes Cardozo's "poetic skills," among them hermeneutics. Weisberg identifies hermeneutics as an important legal technique, and goes on to examine a few of Cardozo's opinions in light of that technique. It is a fascinating discussion, and, if anything, too short. But even Weisberg seems to compartmentalize hermeneutics as a literary tool, though he admits "every legal experience is a hermeneutic experience."

A lawyer who scants hermeneutics does so at great peril. Comprehension of textual meaning is too important and development of interpretive skill too essential to be given less than their due.

Who knows, maybe John Marshall's opinion in *Marbury* v. *Madison* will turn out, on hermeneutical analysis, to be only the culmination of his lifelong search for the Great White Whale.

14

Mencken on Holmes

H. L. MENCKEN, that all-knowing and entertaining commentator on every subject, was born in 1880. On September 12, 1980, his centenary birthday, there were convocations in Baltimore, his home town, as well as in Washington. On that date, even *The New York Times* published an editorial commemorating Mencken's birth. As part of the centenary celebration for this most quintessential of journalists, it is fitting to see what Mencken had to say about law.

Mencken's most interesting comments about law appeared in the May 1930 issue of *The American Mercury*. In that issue, ostensibly reviewing a collection of Justice Holmes's dissents, Mencken announced his own theory of constitutional law. "The very aim of the Constitution," wrote Mencken, "was to keep lawmakers from running amok, and . . . it was the highest duty of the Supreme Court, following *Marbury* v. *Madison*, to safeguard it against their forays." A few paragraphs later, he added, "The important thing is that the Bill of Rights sets forth, in the plainest of plain language, the limits beyond which even legislatures may not go." What the Founding Fathers "sought to hobble was simply the majority."

If Mencken's constitutional theory sounds familiar and respectable, it should. It is, after all, the traditional American theory of judicial review. Mencken's phrasing closely resembles memorable language from opinions of Justices like Black and Douglas. It is not surprising, then, that Mencken, with his stress on the Constitution's protection of individual liberties against encroachment by majorities, viewed himself and his constitutional theory as "Liberal." What is surprising, however, is his criticism of Justice Holmes's credentials as a liberal.

"To call Holmes a Liberal is to make the word meaningless," said Mencken. Taxing Holmes for his opinions against free speech in some Espionage Act cases, Mencken found "it hard to reconcile such notions with any plausible concept of Liberalism." "They may be good law," wrote Mencken, "but it is impossible to see how they can conceivably promote liberty." Yet liberals concluded that Holmes was "a sworn advocate of the rights of man" because, "frantically eager to find at least one judge who was not violently and implacably against them," they seized on certain of Holmes's opinions without examining the rest, including "reactionary opinions which they so politely overlook." It seemed to Mencken that Holmes voted for "the most brutal sort of repression" more often than for the widest freedom.

Certainly Mencken dissented from history's majority opinion in the case of Holmes. Such a minority opinion from Mencken is in keeping with his flair for adopting a position at odds with everyone else. Mencken was always at his best when exploding generally accepted views and knocking heroes off their pedestals. But Mencken's comments on Holmes should not be brushed aside as a mere journalistic display. On the contrary, Mencken's analysis is at times trenchant, useful, and above all, original.

Mencken rightly points out that the "clue to his [i.e., Holmes's] whole jurisprudence" is that Holmes was "an advocate of the rights of lawmakers." Holmes did believe, as Mencken said, that "lawmaking bodies should be free to experiment" and "that the courts should not call a halt upon them until they clearly passed the uttermost bounds of reason." Nonetheless, Mencken suggested that Holmes, viewing the "whole uproar" as an amusing spectacle, apparently had no genuine belief in democracy. When Holmes was disposed to let statutes stand, he was moved, according to Mencken, "far less [by] a positive love of liberty than an amiable and half contemptuous feeling that those who longed for it ought to get a horse-doctor's dose of it, and thereby suffer a really first-rate belly-ache." Mencken read Holmes's deep disposition to let lawmakers have their way as removing any brake on lawmaking and requiring the sacrifice of even the Bill of Rights, which is precisely what Mencken found so objectionable.

But Mencken's objection is way off the mark because it fails to distinguish between laws in the economic and social sphere and laws in the area of civil liberties. Mencken said that the same strict constitutional standards should govern all laws, so as to avoid "loose and elastic" interpretations of constitutional language. But Holmes disagreed, and, anticipating the "preferred-position" theory, allowed lawmakers more leeway to experiment with social and economic measures while scrutinizing more carefully laws abridging civil liberties. In overlooking this important distinction, Mencken resembles, of all people, Felix Frankfurter, one of Holmes's most adoring disciples. Actually, Mencken's criticism of Holmes is much more apt as applied to Frankfurter, who, as a judge, ignored his idol's distinction and was always reluctant to curb legislative will in any area, including the realm of civil liberties.

Although Mencken may have missed a basic distinction, he was far more accurate in other aspects of his analysis of Holmes. With perceptive insight, Mencken enjoined us to stop thinking of Holmes as a liberal, a literateur, a reformer, a sociologist, a prophet, an evangelist, or a metaphysician; and instead to think of him "as something that he undoubtedly was in his Pleistocene youth [Holmes was ninety years old] and probably remained ever after, to wit, a soldier." "On at least three days out of four during his long years on the bench," continued Mencken, "the learned justice remained the soldier—precise, pedantic, unimaginative, even harsh. But on the fourth day a strange amiability overcame him, and a strange impulse to play with heresy, and it was on that fourth day that he acquired his singular repute as a sage."

As one sage considering another, the Sage of Baltimore recognized kindred traits in Holmes. "Once his mood had brought him to this or that judgment," wrote Mencken of Holmes, "the announcement of it was sometimes more than a little affected by purely literary impulses." Surely the same can be said of Mencken's announcements of his own judgments on every subject. And when Mencken described Holmes as a skeptic, "under no illusions about the law," without passionate conviction in popular causes, one cannot help but think Mencken is describing Mencken as well.

For his part, Holmes had some things to say about Mencken, and not all of them bad. In a 1926 letter to Harold Laski, Holmes wrote: "I have read what I didn't care for in him [i.e., Mencken] but I took much pleasure in a volume of *Prejudices.*" More curious is the following excerpt from a 1930 letter to Laski: "My secretary read aloud Mencken's *Treatise on the Gods*—which, as I like M. in some other of his writing, I regretted to think twenty-five or fifty years behind the times. By the by he, as I should have done a year or two ago, treats with summary scorn the notion that Jesus is a myth—but two or three books French and English have made me more respectful to the belief." From a man noted for skepticism in all matters of faith, the 1930 letter is revealing.

Both Mencken and Holmes belong in any American pantheon, but in the last analysis Holmes emerges as the greater of the two. Apart from an early biography of Nietzsche and a book about Shaw, the overwhelming bulk of Mencken's work is critical of his fellow man; funny and witty yes, but neither inspirational nor affirmative. Mencken turned into what the Bible calls a reviler of men, and as a result he faded from popularity during the Depression amid widespread suffering. Mencken's sarcasm and facility with words seduced him. He was left at the station as the train of history moved on.

Holmes, in contrast, grows in stature. His lasting greatness lies not so much in his work as a judge, great as that may have been, as it does in his nonjudicial work, particularly his writings and speeches. Of course, Holmes did important and pioneering work on the bench, and may well have been the greatest judge who ever lived. But judicial theories change and constitutional doctrines are matters of intellectual fashion. The true key to Holmes's continuing attraction is his extraordinary personality, his unflinching attitude to life and law, his inspiring and tolerant cast of mind, and his ability to express himself in language that is apt, concise, and memorable.

So, as we lawyers celebrate the hundredth anniversary of Mencken's birth, it is appropriate to remember that it is also the hundredth anniversary of the publication of *The Common Law* by O. W. Holmes, Jr.

15

Holmes's Common Law
at One Hundred

It was almost exactly a century ago that Oliver Wendell Holmes, Jr. published *The Common Law*. His one and only book, *The Common Law* launched Holmes on his long-lived judicial career and marked a turning point in legal thought. It has impressive qualities that, 100 years later, are worth reconsidering.

We may be better able to grasp these special qualities by contemplating one extraordinary sentence in the book. "The life of the law has not been logic; it has been experience." These thirteen words, in the first paragraph of *The Common Law*, form one of the most riveting sentences in legal literature. Who, having read that provocative sentence, has ever forgotten it? But why is it so memorable?

To penetrate to the heart of a thing—even a little thing such as one sentence—is to experience a special kind of exhilaration. We can approach our task modestly by asking, not whether we can know jurisprudence or the meaning of law, but whether we can know, ultimately and in detail, one sentence of thirteen words. Reflections on a single sentence may provide useful clues to greater understanding of the meaning and significance of Holmes's overall achievement.

The style of the famous sentence has delicacy and economy of phrasing, as well as verbal harmony, all of which give it strength and beauty. Analyzing the sentence further, we see that it, like almost all memorable writing, is meant to be read aloud, and that it depends on several rhetorical devices.

First, note the alliteration. "Life," "law," and "logic" all occur in the same clause. This alliterative effect adds to the impact of the words. The repetitive "l" sound lingers in the mind's ear.

Coupled with alliteration is Holmes's use of short, easily understood words. Of the thirteen words in the sentence, all but two are small common words of one syllable. And the two words that have more than one syllable are "logic" and "experience," both of which are simple yet absolutely key to the sense of the passage. None of the words is jargon. Anyone can read the sentence and understand it.

The effect grows with cadence and rhythm. We can see these qualities by breaking down the sentence: The *life/* of the *law/* has *not* been *logic/* it has been *experience.* The four phrases in the sentence progressively increase in number of syllables and all end with a stressed final word. There is an artful build-up to the last crucial word.

The passage also makes skillful use of antithesis. It sets "logic" and "experience" in contrast with each other. The juxtaposition of "logic" and "experience" alerts us to the contours of Holmes's daring thesis. Holmes's use of opposition highlights, in a lasting way, the essential point he is trying to make.

Holmes's essential point is itself an antithesis, an attack on prevailing authority. Holmes broke with the accepted way of viewing how legal rules are formed. In the place of sterile deductive reasoning, Holmes called for sensitive analysis and weighing of competing policy considerations.

Holmes's passage about law, logic, and experience is, in substance, a microcosm of the universe of Holmes's legal thought. In style, it is typical of the rest of the book and vividly illustrates Holmes's attention, not only to *what* he wrote but to *how* he wrote.

But of course there is more to *The Common Law* than one sentence. Holmes explains his highly imaginative theme again and again, in language that echoes down through the years:

"The felt necessities of the time, the prevalent moral and political theories, intuitions of public policy, avowed or unconscious, even the prejudices which judges share with their fellow-men, have had a good deal more to do than the syllogism in determining the rules by which men should be governed. The law embodies the story of a nation's development through many centuries, and it cannot be dealt with as if it contained only the axioms and corollaries of a book of mathematics."

"The very considerations which judges most rarely mention, and always with an apology, are the secret root from which the law draws all the juices of life. I mean, of course considerations of what is expedient for the community concerned."

"The first requirement of a sound body of law is that it should correspond with the actual feelings and demands of the community, whether right or wrong."

Holmes's stress on the limitations inherent in the logical method as applied to law entitles *The Common Law* to an important place in the broader history of ideas. When Holmes talks of the "failure of all theories which consider the law only from its formal side" of logical deduction, he is frankly acknowledging the crucial role played by irrational forces. Considered from the perspective of intellectual history, *The Common Law* may be one of the first examples of the modern antirationalist movement, typified by Nietzsche in philosophy and Freud in psychology. Toward the end of the nineteenth and beginning of the twentieth centuries, each of these thinkers and others rebelled against the formal rationalist systems dominating their fields.

In exposing the limitations of pure rationalism, Holmes and others were revolutionary thinkers. They prompted whole new branches of study and provoked reappraisal of existing philosophies. It was the lot of these intellectual rebels to cut loose from the moorings of the past and set a course on uncharted waters, to be sailed by those who came after them. Their work has in large part shaped our intellectual climate.

They gained what Holmes elsewhere called "the secret isolated joy of the thinker, who knows that, a hundred years after he is dead and forgotten, men who never heard of him will be moving to the measure of his thought—the subtle rapture of a postponed power."

Ability to stand the test of time is one attribute of a classic. To be a work of enduring significance, a piece of writing should be capable of being read with profit more than once, and should yield many interpretations on many levels. And if it is part of a larger movement of intellectual history, then we know we are dealing with a work of art.

The Common Law is a complex work of art, for Holmes was a literary artist as well as a consummate legal philosopher. It does not spoil such a work of art to analyze it as closely as we have done. It helps us to pierce more deeply into the rich meaning of Holmes's philosophy of law, and it allows the very rare privilege of watching—a century later—the workings of a great man's mind.

16

The Theorems of Holmes and Gödel

DURING this centennial of Holmes's *Common Law*, we should think about the limited utility of logic in the law. That was, after all, the main theme of Holmes's great book. His theme can serve as the basis for exploring the process of legal reasoning and even of reasoning in general. But Holmes's theme cuts deeper than he knew. It anticipates the most startling findings of twentieth century logic.

Logic implies certainty and consistency. Yet Holmes accepted uncertainty and inconsistency in the law. "The language of judicial decision," he wrote in *The Path of the Law*, "is mainly the language of logic. And the logical method and form flatter that longing for certainty and for repose which is in every human mind. But certainty generally is illusion, and repose is not the destiny of man."

Explaining "the failure of all theories which consider the law only from its formal side," Holmes wrote in *The Common Law*, "The truth is, that the law is always approaching, and never reaching, consistency . . . It will become entirely consistent only when it ceases to grow."

For Holmes, then, certainty and consistency were not the ultimate values in legal thinking.

We cannot reach certainty in the law because it is not

there to be reached. According to Jerome Frank, the quest for certainty in the law springs from an immature craving for the predictability and authoritativeness of a father figure. It supposes that law is an imperturbable machine which we view from the outside. That picture is false. Law is a network of intertwining relationships and we are among those relationships. Law, Holmes wrote, "is forever adopting new principles from life."

Uncertainty means ambiguity, and ambiguity is necessary for growth in the law. The language of the law cannot, thankfully, be freed from ambiguity. Law would come to a standstill if every ambiguity were resolved, for there would be nothing left to interpret. The strictly logical and formal rendering of law is the right attitude in a discipline that is closed; it is clearly the wrong one when a discipline is still growing.

A logical construction that has been made to contain only the existing facts and relations cannot accommodate new ideas. If your definition of a contract, say, is operationally or logically exact, in the sense of a formal writing, then it may be too narrow; it leaves you no room to discover that a contract may be oral or even implicit. The concepts of any growing field must be richer and more pliable than any logical construction from the sum of its known facts.

The concepts that form the critical words in the vocabulary of the law mean much the same thing to every user, and yet they do not mean the same thing. If they did, then no one could start to think of a fresh concept. The right of privacy did not mean the same thing to Brandeis and Warren that it had meant to lawyers before them. Freedom of speech did not mean the same thing to Justice Black that it had meant to Holmes, and it meant more to Holmes with his clear and present danger test than it had meant to his conventional predecessors. A past generation uncovered in the phrase *due process of law* a substantive meaning hidden to all those who had used it since the Magna Carta. Imagination takes advantage of ambiguity in the language of the law.

Of course it is true that when judges write, they try to rid their language of ambiguity and make it exact. This is what Holmes meant when he referred to "the language of judicial decision" being cast in "the language of logic." But we should not confuse the language in which law is made with that in which it is explained—the thought with its formal communication. The aim of a judicial opinion (or a legal brief for that matter) is to display the conclusion definitively, and place it in the existing framework of legal axioms and theorems. But the thinking lawyer does not have to accept the present state of the law as closed, and its exposition as complete.

The ideal of much legal theory—to uncover an ultimate and comprehensive set of axioms from which all legal phenomena could be shown to follow by deductive steps—is hopeless. This insight might be called Holmes's Theorem, and it is his most important contribution to jurisprudence. Its significance, however, goes beyond legal philosophy. It presages the most fundamental discoveries of modern logic.

In 1931, exactly fifty years after Holmes's Theorem was published, a young Austrian mathematician, Kurt Gödel, discovered another theorem with enormous repercussions. Up to then, there had been many attempts by mathematicians and philosophers to mechanize the thought processes of reasoning, always stressing the completeness and consistency of any logical system. Gödel proved that a logical system that has any richness can never be complete, nor guaranteed to be consistent. Gödel's Theorem was electrifying. It reshaped the foundations of mathematics by showing that every axiomatic system of any richness is subject to severe limitations, whose incidence can be neither foreseen nor avoided. Only an axiom which introduces a contradiction can make a system complete, and in doing so makes it completely useless.

The implications of Gödel's Theorem for any theory of law have been ignored for too long, despite Holmes's prescient anticipation of them. Every theory of law is incomplete, and in that sense is approximate; simply as a logical machine, it cannot cover all the changing phenomena of society. It therefore follows, not merely in practice but in principle, that the system must be enlarged from time to time by adding new axioms, which cannot be foreseen or proved to be free from contradiction. This is what Holmes meant when he wrote, "The law is always approaching, and never reaching consistency" because it "is forever adopting new principles from life."

How does the outstanding lawyer come to propose such a decisive new axiom or principle, while less imaginative minds go on tinkering with the old system? How did John Marshall leap to conceive the theory of judicial review? What moved the Warren Court to make equality of legislative apportionment not a consequence but an axiom in the construction of a representative democracy? The answer is the creative process.

The step by which a new axiom is added cannot itself be mechanized. It is a free play of the mind, an invention outside the logical processes. This is the central act of imagination in law, and it is in all respects like any similar act in art or literature or science. The creative process is much the same in all fields.

Holmes's creativity is shown by his perceiving, while focusing on law, the limitations that circumscribe *any* axiomatic and deductive system of a reasonable richness. The announcement of Holmes's Theorem in 1881 foreshadowed some of the most remarkable developments of twentieth century thought. Holmes, like Gödel, intuitively understood that new theorems need to be incorporated as added axioms in a system.

17

The Changing Reputation
of Louis Brandeis

Reputation is a changeable quality. It is important to most people: as Shakespeare says, "Good name in man or woman . . . is the immediate jewel of their souls." But reputation, when based on public opinion, can vary as that opinion varies. When based on facts supposed to be true, reputation can change if different facts come to light. As a result of startling new facts, we are witnessing a change in the reputation of a major figure in American jurisprudence: Louis D. Brandeis, Associate Justice of the Supreme Court from 1916 to 1939.

I

For decades, Brandeis has enjoyed a reputation as one of our greatest Supreme Court Justices. Exquisite technical abilities as a lawyer and judge played a role in earning Brandeis his wonderful reputation, but his legal skills explain only part of his stature. After all, there were other, equally skilled jurists from Brandeis's time who are far less admired today than Brandeis. The key to the high esteem for Brandeis lies in two qualities: the allure of the social and political views that he voiced, mostly in dissent, as law, and in his universally admired personal integrity. Those were the qualities that made Brandeis special.

Brandeis's social and political views are still attractive to many of us. Coming to maturity in the late 1800s, Brandeis was the first Progressive appointed to the Court. As a practicing lawyer, he took part in many efforts and court cases for better working conditions, shorter hours for labor, less concentration of wealth, more economic competition, and in general most of the Progressive goals. With the exception of one Justice, the Court that Brandeis joined was neither distinguished nor memorable for its concern for economic and social realities, Progressive ideology, or even intellectual ability. Against such a flat background, Brandeis was bound to stand out.

The exception was Oliver Wendell Holmes, Jr. But even Holmes, at least the intellectual equal of Brandeis, cannot fairly be regarded as a Progressive. Holmes was too much of a philosophical skeptic to believe in the Idea of Progress or in human perfectibility. Holmes's reluctance to overturn social and economic legislation stemmed more from his limited notion of judicial review than from agreement with the aims of the legislation at issue. If the people's representatives wanted to tinker with social and economic arrangements, Holmes saw nothing in the Constitution to stop them.

Brandeis did his best to convert Holmes into a believer. He continually prodded Holmes to become more sensitive to current social and economic issues. In this campaign, Brandeis sent to Holmes many books filled with facts on such issues. For his part, Holmes found such reading tedious and not at all to his liking. He could not bring himself actually to believe in what he pejoratively referred to as "upward and onward" efforts. Brandeis's efforts to convert Holmes led Max Lerner, in his excellent introductory essay to *The Mind and Faith of Justice Holmes*, to conclude that, "Brandeis was Holmes's conscience."

In a larger sense, though, Brandeis was for years the conscience of the entire Court. He steadfastly opposed the conservative social and economic views then dominating the Court. To allow play in society's joints for other views, Brandeis the believer (together with Holmes the skeptic) wrote some of the most moving and memorable lines ever written in defense of freedom of expression. What law student has not felt his heart go faster when reading for the first time Brandeis's concurring opinion in *Whitney* v. *California?*

Those who won our independence believed that the final end of the State was to make men free to develop their faculties; and that in its government the deliberative forces should prevail over the arbitrary. They valued liberty both as an end and as a means. They believed liberty to be the secret of happiness and courage to be the secret of liberty. They believed that freedom to think as you will and to speak as you think are means indispensable to the discovery and spread of political truth; that without free speech and assembly discussion would be futile; that with them, discussion affords ordinarily adequate protection against the dissemination of noxious doctrine; that the greatest menace to freedom is an inert people; that public discussion is a political duty; and that this should be a fundamental principle of the American government. They recognized the risks to which all human institutions are subject. But they knew that order cannot be secured merely through fear of punishment for its infraction; that it is hazardous to discourage thought, hope and imagination; that fear breeds repression; that repression breeds hate; that hate menaces stable government; that the path of safety lies in the opportunity to discuss freely supposed grievances and proposed remedies; and that the fitting remedy for evil counsels is good ones. Believing in the power of reason as applied through public discussion, they eschewed silence coerced by law—the argument of force in its worst form. Recognizing the occasional tyrannies of governing major-

ities, they amended the Constitution so that free speech and assembly should be guaranteed.

Those lines, with their haunting rhythms and cadences,
will live as long as freedom of thought is cherished. Anyone, particularly a lawyer, who can read those glorious passages without his eyes puddling simply has no sense of
what this country is all about. They show that, while most
of Brandeis's writing is only crisp and businesslike, at
times he reached the absolute heights with the power of
his language.

Similarly, Brandeis's dissent in *Olmstead* (in which he
viewed unauthorized wiretapping as unconstitutional) and
his seminal law review article on the right of privacy are
bright beacons. If these achievements were not enough,
Brandeis's entire social and economic philosophy, his bedrock belief in competition together with human dignity,
his lifetime of effort to better human working conditions—
all these would assure Brandeis of a secure place as an authentic American hero.

Brandeis was able to bring off his role as judicial preacher
largely because of his legendary personal integrity. Although Holmes did not agree with all of Brandeis's political
objectives, he undoubtedly was moved by what Max Lerner
calls Brandeis's "complete integrity . . . by his ethical
sense, by his almost agonizing determination to do the
right thing." According to Lerner, when Brandeis left the
Holmeses' house, the Justice would say to Mrs. Holmes,
"There goes a good man." What Holmes felt, others felt
too. An ascetic in his personal life, Brandeis was a moralist
with definite ideas of right and wrong, particularly in the
realm of social and economic realities. He has been perceived as an exemplar of personal self-control and judicial

self-restraint, observing every jurisdictional and procedural limitation on the Supreme Court's authority. It was Brandeis who, in counseling against intruding on the prerogatives of other branches of government, wrote: "The most important thing we do is not doing." As a consequence, Brandeis has always been pictured as a model of judicial virtue with rigorous standards of propriety—until now.

II

The very qualities that were the source of Brandeis's enviable reputation, however, have now come under scholarly scrutiny. Brandeis appreciated good scholarship: In one of the most important cases of this century, *Erie Railroad Co.* v. *Tompkins,* Brandeis's opinion for the Court overruled a hundred years of precedent because of what Brandeis referred to as "the research of a competent scholar." Thanks to two books by what Brandeis would have called "competent scholars," we may be on the brink of overturning fifty years of received wisdom about Brandeis's reputation. For we now know that while on the bench Brandeis engaged in behavior strikingly at odds with the traditional ideal of a disinterested judge. In his 1981 book *The Enigma of Felix Frankfurter,* H. N. Hirsch first disclosed that Brandeis paid money to Frankfurter to promote Brandeis's political views while Brandeis was a Supreme Court Justice and Frankfurter was a law professor at Harvard. In 1982, Bruce Allen Murphy published *The Brandeis/Frankfurter Connection,* in which he detailed the complete story of the extrajudicial activities of both men.

The disclosures in the two recent books are revealing. On the basis of newly discovered evidence that seems incontrovertible, the two books provide the facts of Brandeis's extraordinary political activities after going on the bench. Those activities ranged from secretly hiring a prominent stalking-horse (i.e., Frankfurter) to publicize and implement his political programs, to using a network of acquaintances to influence political decisions, to closely participating in proposing and drafting of New Deal legislation, and, when his legislative proposals were not followed, to eventually threatening executive officials that he would use his judicial power to hold competing legislation unconstitutional.

Each of these activities is fascinating in its own right; together they provide a new picture of Brandeis's judicial temperament. They cast doubt on the conventional picture of Brandeis as a model of judicial virtue.

From hitherto unavailable private correspondence between the principals, it is clear that between 1916 and 1938 Brandeis, while on the Supreme Court, paid Felix Frankfurter $56,000 for carrying out political and social activities at Brandeis's request. In the years 1917 to 1924, Brandeis paid Frankfurter an annual retainer of $1,000, in 1925 $2,500, and from 1926 to 1938 $3,500. In terms of 1981 dollars, the $3,500 Brandeis paid Frankfurter each year from 1926 to 1938 was worth between $19,000 and $26,000, depending on the year involved. In return for these secret and substantial payments (Frankfurter's yearly salary as a Harvard law professor during this time varied between $6,000 and $10,000), Frankfurter acted as Brandeis's lieutenant, surrogate and agent for proposing and supporting political reforms and influencing the course of political decisions.

Through Frankfurter and on his own, Brandeis used a wide range of governmental and nongovernmental contacts to affect decisionmaking outside the judicial branch. He counseled Presidents, cabinet members, senators, and congressmen on how to cope with the most pressing political problems, even suggesting and commenting on specific legislation. He sometimes used Frankfurter to draft legislation to correct new Supreme Court decisions Brandeis thought were wrong. He surreptitiously had Frankfurter and the best of Frankfurter's students at Harvard write law review articles advocating his point of view on legal questions, which Brandeis then cited as authority in his Supreme Court opinions.

By far the most astounding revelations concern Brandeis's intense involvement in the New Deal. Perhaps it was only natural for Brandeis, the aging Progressive, to be interested in FDR's social and economic reforms. But Brandeis was more than merely interested; by February 1933 Brandeis had, in letters to Frankfurter, mapped out detailed plans for changing and revitalizing the American economy. Brandeis's plan had four aspects: huge public works projects, vast tax revisions, reforms in financial and banking practices, and, to carry out these reforms, staffing the government with able lawyers having "the right attitude." Basically, Brandeis wanted to see a more competitive economy in which individual states played a large role. The task of advocating Brandeis's pro-competitive and decentralized plans within the Administration fell to Frankfurter and Frankfurter's protégés, including Thomas Corcoran and Benjamin Cohen.

Brandeis's views reflected only one of two very different sets of programs being pressed on FDR at the start. In sharp contrast to Brandeis's views about the need for more competition and decentralization, Roosevelt's "Brain Trust" of Columbia University professors Rexford Tugwell, Raymond Moley and Adolf Berle favored bigness in federal government and less competitive business practices. Described as "social planners" and "collectivists," they wanted to centralize the economy under large-scale national programs involving cooperation among government, agriculture, and business sectors. The struggle for influence between the Brandeis-Frankfurter group, on the one hand, and the Tugwell-Moley group, on the other, pushed Brandeis beyond the ordinary bounds of judicial propriety.

To make his political and social views prevail, Brandeis used several methods. He discussed details of prospective legislation and executive policies with Frankfurter and a few higher-level New Deal officials. With Frankfurter's help, he was able to place scores of lawyers "with the right attitude" (often former students of Frankfurter) throughout the Roosevelt Administration. Both Brandeis and Frankfurter lobbied intensively for their programs.

So involved was Brandeis that, while sitting as a Justice of the Supreme Court, he played a major role in drafting specific legislation. The successful legislative drafting team of Corcoran and Cohen frequently met with Brandeis at his apartment to discuss problems with possible solutions. After these meetings, Brandeis would send specific legislative proposals to Frankfurter, who would then forward the proposals to FDR. The President would in turn give the ideas to Corcoran and Cohen for action. Corcoran and Cohen, who well knew where the proposals originated, then drafted the actual legislation. During this process, Brandeis was quite active in advising the draftsmen, particularly regarding financial reform measures.

Despite these efforts, the fact is that during the first years of the New Deal Brandeis's ideas lost out to those of the "social planners" and "collectivists." The early part of the first Roosevelt Administration saw many new federal agencies trying to control the entire American economy.

The Agricultural Adjustment Act and the National Industrial Recovery Act became law and centralized a national economy without competition, much to Brandeis's distress. Other of FDR's programs fell far short of Brandeis's proposal for a massive public works program. Displeased but hoping for a change, Brandeis warned Administration officials of the serious problems generated by their centralized programs. When no change came, Brandeis unsheathed the one potent weapon he had up to then kept in his scabbard.

Starting around April 1934, Brandeis, incredibly, threatened the Administration that if it did not follow his ideas he would vote to hold New Deal legislation unconstitutional. Brandeis let Administration officials know "he was declaring war" on the New Deal. After one meeting with Jerome Frank and Adolf Berle on the evils of "bigness" inherent in the AAA and the NRA, Brandeis, according to Berle, warned he "had gone along with the legislation up to now, but that unless he could see some reversal of the big business trend, he was disposed to hold the government control legislation unconstitutional from now on." Nor was Brandeis's threat idle; it was a threat he would make good on. In 1935, Brandeis joined a unanimous Court in three decisions declaring unconstitutional first Roosevelt's dismissal of a Federal Trade Commissioner, then the Frazier-Lemke Act (a farm mortgage relief measure), and finally the NRA in the *Schechter* case. Immediately following the decisions, Cohen and Corcoran were called to the Court where Brandeis told them:

You have heard our three decisions. They change everything. . . . The President has been living in a fool's paradise. . . . Everything that you [the Administration] have been doing must be changed.

Everything must be considered most carefully in light of these decisions by a unanimous Court.

Surely this scene is one of the most remarkable in Supreme Court history.

III

It was only natural that publication of these new facts would cause controversy. A few months after *The Brandeis/Frankfurter Connection* came out, *The New Republic* published an article by Yale law professor Robert Cover entitled "The Framing of Justice Brandeis." Professor Cover's article has emerged as the most complete attack on the scholarship on which the new facts are based. But it only serves to show how much emotional resistance there is to any criticism, however much justified, of our cherished heroes.

No hero should be exempt from scrutiny. The inventor of the "Brandeis brief" would be the first to agree that conventional wisdom and belief must be tested by "facts" and "reality." There is an obligation, an obligation that Brandeis acted on all his life, to face squarely the actual facts, and, in light of them, to draw our own conclusions. To do less would dishonor Brandeis in the worst possible way: it would erect an indefensible double standard for the Brandeis method by carving out an exception for its originator.

Applying the Brandeis method to Brandeis himself leaves little dispute about the essential facts.

As to the Frankfurter retainer itself, Professor Cover concedes that "it is clear that regular payments were made for a number of years." There is also no dispute that Frankfurter carried out many different activities for Brandeis during this period. Professor Cover disputes not the facts but the "condemnatory tone and the conspiracy thesis" of the recent revelations.

Professor Cover also comes forward with no evidence to refute the proof that Brandeis threatened to declare New Deal legislation unconstitutional if his legislative advice were not followed. Quite to the contrary, Professor Cover concedes, referring to the extraordinary threat, that two different contemporary documents as well as later oral recollections "convey the same tone." Absent hard evidence to support his position, he is reduced to arguing that, "it is possible to reconstruct the events in a number of ways," and asserting that such a threat "would have been out of character" for Brandeis. Professor Cover also characterizes the sources of the new evidence as ambiguous, and he argues that any conclusions can be tentative only. But, short of a smoking gun—a document signed by Brandeis and containing the threat, for example—evidence about events in the past will always have some ambiguity and all conclusions are provisional and subject to modification in view of later discovered facts.

Professor Cover does not even mention what is by far the most curious incident recounted in *The Brandeis/Frankfurter Connection*. The incident, in which Brandeis called in Cohen and Corcoran immediately after the Court had declared the NRA unconstitutional, goes unchallenged in Cover's article. From the existing evidence, we can only conclude that the incident occurred—until evidence to the contrary comes to light.

With respect to Brandeis's participating in the legislative process, Cover accuses Bruce Allen Murphy of "misuse of evidence." Focusing on certain minor correspondence, Cover says it fails conclusively to prove Brandeis's involvement. Yet Cover himself agrees that it is "generally accepted" that Brandeis was "the guiding spirit, perhaps the dominant influence" in the federal legislative pact passed in 1934–1935. Nor does Cover refute that Cohen and Corcoran would frequently meet with Brandeis in his apartment to discuss government problems and proposed solutions, and that, "[f]ollowing these conferences, the justice would send his specific legislative proposals to Frankfurter." In view of this uncontradicted statement, Cover's criticism appears to be unjustified. After all, what was a Supreme Court justice doing sending specific legislative proposals to a presidential advisor?

What we have, then, is not so much a disagreement as to basic facts, but a dispute over how these facts should be judged or evaluated. Yet even here there are significant points of general agreement about the applicable standards. For instance, Professor Cover concedes that, "Certainly many of us would condemn as unethical a judge sitting upon the constitutionality of a law that he had helped draft and administer." He also agrees that private threats to declare legislation unconstitutional if his advice is not followed constitutes "misuse of his power as a judge." Elsewhere he writes, "Extrajudicial political activity by judges will always lie within contested terrain."

Given the facts as best we know them, we must grapple with the issues raised by Brandeis's behavior. The heart of the issue is the role of the Supreme Court in American government. It is not just a matter of a vague concept of separation of powers. Rather, for Supreme Court justices to become involved in the hurly-burly of the political process threatens the acceptance of the Court's position as ultimate arbiter. If the Court is to exercise the power of judicial review, it must appear to be above the political fray.

To be sure, more research and scholarship are needed to verify the facts and establish the truth. And we must always be careful to avoid the historicist fallacy of interpreting events of another era in terms of today's perhaps different standards. But all the same, we would be intellectually dishonest if we brushed aside and ignored the revelations that have come to light about Brandeis. If even a good man like Brandeis is susceptible to such temptation, we need to know that.

My own suspicion is that many of us find the evidence hard to swallow because we revere Brandeis so much. To criticize a hero is risky business. But fair and balanced criticism is essential. It will not do for us to say, as I think Professor Cover is saying: "I can't believe it; therefore it must not be true." We cannot wish away the facts.

IV

The facts require us to reevaluate Brandeis's behavior as a judge. They put in serious doubt the persona of complete judicial propriety placed on Brandeis by received wisdom. They raise basic questions about the limits of judicial propriety. They compel us to ask how Brandeis, admittedly a good man, could have violated his own strictures against interfering with other branches of government. They call to mind criticism of Brandeis during his confirmation hearings as lacking in "judicial temperament." Were the critics right?

How can we even begin to explain Brandeis's extraordinary behavior, his disregard for the proprieties and something as basic as the separation of powers? Although other Supreme Court Justices have engaged in extrajudicial activities, none did so in Brandeis's way; nor were any of them Louis Brandeis. Brandeis was too sensitive an individual not to realize what he was doing or that it was wrong. The secrecy that has shrouded his activities for some fifty years strongly suggests that he realized both. Brandeis's conduct is particularly puzzling in view of his frequent comments about the dangers of violating the separation of powers. How could Brandeis ignore his own warnings?

The most likely answer is that Brandeis was too passionate. Throughout his life, as crusading lawyer and moralizing judge, Brandeis had definite ideas and goals, clear dreams for remaking American life. By the time FDR became President, Brandeis was seventy-three years old and anxious to realize his long-cherished visions. Time was running out for the aging Brandeis, and so he did what other passionate believers have done in the past: he tried to bring about the results he so desperately wanted by other than normal means. Toward the close of his life, Brandeis reverted to his earlier role as zealous advocate rather than disinterested judge, making the end justify the means.

This explanation is, unfortunately, a common one in history. Good people who believe in a cause become frustrated at delay and give short shrift to the means used to accomplish the ends. Such people plan and carry out holy wars and inquisitions, revolutions and new social orders. Such people are so sure they are right that they subordinate the normal process of change to the importance of achieving the goals of change.

Brandeis, of all people, should have known better. He should have curbed his desire to see his precious reforms carried out. The claims of process are great. It was Brandeis who in 1928 wrote in *Olmstead* v. *United States*, a wiretapping case, these celebrated lines:

Our Government is the potent, omnipresent teacher. For good or for ill, it teaches the whole people by its example. Crime is contagious. If the Government becomes a lawbreaker, it breeds contempt for law; it invites every man to become a law unto himself; it invites anarchy. To declare that in the administration of the criminal law the end justifies the means—to declare that the Government may commit crimes in order to secure the conviction of a private criminal—would bring terrible retribution. Against that pernicious doctrine this Court should resolutely set its face.

As in the administration of the criminal law, so too at the highest levels of judicial administration. Supreme Court Justices are potent teachers by their example. If a respected Supreme Court Justice ignores the separation of powers, he breeds contempt for law and the judicial process itself.

It is still too early to tell how much Brandeis's reputation will be affected by the revelations of his inappropriate conduct. None of the new facts changes our estimate of his intelligence or the power of his judicial opinions. Perhaps the most notable result will be to bring Brandeis down to human size. He was a man with foibles, who believed too much in his own vision of the "good" to stay his hand when he saw an opportunity to accomplish the result. But in our system of government, the *process* of decisionmaking is sometimes more important than the *results* of any particular decision.

Oliver Wendell Holmes, Jr., that mustachioed old skeptic, would have enjoyed all this. Wherever he is, he is probably smiling to himself. Here is his good friend Brandeis hoist by his own petard. No doubt Holmes is thinking to himself that Brandeis should have spent less time being Holmes's conscience and more time developing a conscience of his own.

18

Felix Frankfurter

FELIX Frankfurter was a most puzzling Supreme Court Justice. Equipped with superb technical skills and steeped in constitutional history, Frankfurter sat on the Court for twenty-three years, but his performance on the bench somehow fell short of its great promise. As a Justice, he personified The Lawyer: hypertechnical, longwinded, persnickety, more concerned with process than with substance. His advocacy of judicial restraint was maddening to those who admired his civil libertarian crusades before he went on the Court.

Now there is no doubt about it. Felix Frankfurter was a tragic figure. This is not to say that Frankfurter was not brilliant or learned; he was both. But his brilliance and learning—together with his many other virtues—only underscore the basic tragedy of his life: the failure to realize his potential greatness.

Such a verdict is not rendered lightly, nor without regard for the opinions of other people. But rendered it must be, especially in view of the evidence contained in Frankfurter's *Diaries* and in a recent psychobiography of him.

I

The *Diaries* show the dimensions of Frankfurter's tragedy in Frankfurter's own words. Before now we have had thousands and thousands of Frankfurter's words to study—books, articles, letters, and judicial opinions. Based on these other writings, Professor Fred Rodell concluded in 1955: "Felix Frankfurter, technical successor to the magnificent Holmes and the great Cardozo, stands out as the New Deal Court's most controversial and unhappy figure, its most tragically wasted brilliant mind." Frankfurter's *Diaries* leave Rodell's judgment undisturbed.

What emerges most clearly from the *Diaries* is Frankfurter's capacity for projecting his own personal shortcomings and inadequacies on to other people. For example, Frankfurter's *Diaries* contain severe criticisms of fellow Justice William O. Douglas as a two-faced flatterer and manipulator of men. Yet Frankfurter himself confesses that he would flatter FDR and Chief Justice Harlan F. Stone, when in fact such flattery was insincere. As Joseph P. Lash notes in his introductory essay, "The courtier-like expressions in some of his [i.e. Frankfurter's] letters to Roosevelt are melancholy testimony to an eagerness to please that went beyond loyalty."

So too with Frankfurter's criticism of Douglas's political ambitions during the 1940s. Frankfurter explains many of Douglas's judicial votes in terms of Douglas's desire to become the Democratic candidate for President or Vice-President in 1944 and 1948. But Frankfurter, upon ascending to the Supreme Court, was not averse to playing his own game of politics. Much to the contrary, the *Diaries* corroborate that Frankfurter was the very prototype of a Justice who continued to advise the President who had appointed him.

In one passage Frankfurter describes persons in the State Department, but the mind's eye sees how well the same description fits Frankfurter himself. "[H]e is like so many people, who have not had the advantages of the so-called well born, but wish they had them, more 'Grotty' than the men who actually went to Groton."

There are long *Diary* entries complaining about the way Douglas and Hugo Black tried to dominate the Court, but these complaints sound more than anything else like sour grapes from a sore loser. Frankfurter often writes of how humble he is, and how he can only be guided by his "poor lights." But his assumed humility is a pose, a sanctimonious cloak for bitterness. For in other entries, Frankfurter brags arrogantly about his superior knowledge of law and the Supreme Court.

Frankfurter's chauvinist attitude toward women ("How deeply women sink themselves in others—someone must be the object of their devotion.") found expression in a 1948 majority opinion which upheld a Michigan statute providing that no woman could obtain a bartender's license unless she was "the wife or daughter of the male owner" of a licensed liquor establishment.

Supplementing these insights into personality is a fine biographical essay by Mr. Lash. What makes the essay so good and interesting is not the recounting of the facts and events in Frankfurter's life; those are fairly well known. Rather it is Lash's attempt to understand and explain Frankfurter's disappointing performance on the Court.

Frankfurter, Lash notes, idolized Justice Holmes and invoked his name in support of wholesale judicial restraint. But Lash rightly points out that Holmes had differentiated between regulation of economic matters and regulation of civil liberties. "To assert that the Court had no larger function in the protection of civil liberties than of property rights was a fateful refinement in Frankfurter's position. . . . This refinement uncoupled him from the locomotive of history. . . . Invoking the hallowed name of Holmes he pushed the doctrine of judicial restraint to an extreme that violated the spirit of Holmes."

As a result Frankfurter left a spotty record on the Court. At times capable of great insight and felicitous expression, he was not the author of many memorable opinions on substantive issues. Again and again, he would avoid such issues—and perpetuate social wrongs—by relying on the "passive virtues."

Mr. Lash has done a service to history by publishing Frankfurter's *Diaries.* In addition to the portrait of Frankfurter the man, the reader is treated to an unusually candid picture of infighting among Justices of the Supreme Court. It is healthy to know that our institutions are not monoliths.

II

When Frankfurter's personal diaries were published in 1975, we saw just how bitterly he felt about some of the things happening on the Court. Now we know why.

H. N. Hirsch's book *The Enigma of Felix Frankfurter* is a psychological study. Its "central hypothesis" is that Frankfurter "can only be understood politically if we understand him psychologically, and that we can understand him psychologically as representing a textbook case of a neurotic personality: someone whose self-image is overblown and yet, at the same time, essential to his sense of well being." According to Hirsch, who teaches government at Harvard, "There is a nearly precise fit between Frankfurter and the neurotic personality type."

Hirsch bases his diagnosis of Frankfurter as neurotic on patterns running through key periods of Frankfurter's life. Frankfurter's period of identity formation was, in Hirsch's view, both overly prolonged and torturously difficult. He did not form a coherent self-image until his mid-thirties, after a period of intense psychological stress. This delay was due to a fundamental ambiguity in his choice of an identity and the emotional complications attached to that ambiguity. His personal life had been rocked by the death of his father and by a long and difficult courtship. It was not until Frankfurter, age thirty-seven, went to the Paris Peace Conference in 1919 that he thought of himself as a success, particularly in manipulating people.

After Paris, Frankfurter returned to Harvard to marry and to start a long tenure as a law professor that would last until his appointment to the Supreme Court in 1939. For twenty years, Frankfurter applied the style that was a success in Paris, a style that included flattery and behind-the-scenes maneuvering. With respect to his relationships at Harvard, to public events, and to the New Deal, Frankfurter's style worked.

By this time, Frankfurter had developed an exaggerated self-image. Resting on an arrogant self-importance, this self-image was constantly reinforced by two decades of accumulating success. He saw himself as dominating every personal and professional situation in which he found himself. He felt he could take command of a situation, that he could overcome opposition. This constant "winning" was necessary to Frankfurter, to prove to himself that he measured up to his self-image. Frankfurter's ability to defeat opponents was crucial to his psychological functioning. It ill prepared him for his role as a Supreme Court Justice.

Frankfurter's initial years on the Supreme Court represented his first confrontation with a sustained challenge to his self-image in a field he considered his own. The challenge was all the more upsetting because Frankfurter undoubtedly thought the Supreme Court an arena in which he was superbly qualified to triumph. Successful as an academic, liberal spokesman and activist, and presidential advisor, Frankfurter had every reason to look forward to his time as a Supreme Court Justice. But, for the first time in his life, Frankfurter was faced with a situation in which he could not triumph, in which he could not overcome opposition to his policies and goals. The other Justices, strong-willed and intelligent, resented Frankfurter's attempts to influence and lead them.

The crucial point in the relationships between Frankfurter and the rest of the Court came in the flag-salute cases. In *Gobitis*, which came up at the end of the 1939 term, the question was whether children of Jehovah's Witnesses could be required to salute the flag in school. The Witnesses claimed the flag salute was forbidden by their religion—because it constituted worship of a graven image—and thus violated their right to free exercise of religion under the First Amendment. In an "eloquent and moving" opinion for eight members of the Court, Frankfurter ruled against the Witnesses. Frankfurter's *Gobitis* opinion brought together his dearly held belief that the Court should defer to majority rule (even when intolerant or repressive), his ardent patriotism, his belief in the power and importance of national symbols, his belief in the irrelevance of religious affiliation, and an opportunity to prove himself a "disinterested" jurist.

Barely three years later, the Court reversed itself. Presented with the same facts as *Gobitis*, the Court reached exactly the opposite conclusion in *Barnette*. In ringing phrases, Justice Jackson's majority opinion in *Barnette* defended a broad concept of freedom of belief. But for Frankfurter, the eight-to-one majority of *Gobitis* had gradually slipped away until Frankfurter was left with only

Roberts and Reed in dissent in *Barnette.* "The result," in Hirsch's words, "was a long, personal, emotional opinion, one that hardened Frankfurter's stand on the question of judicial review and thereby set the tenor of his entire philosophy of law."

The philosophy of law expressed by Frankfurter in *Barnette* amounted to a definite ideological commitment. *Barnette* marked a clear transition for Frankfurter and the Court. The remainder of Frankfurter's tenure on the Court was, in a sense, devoted to refighting the battle of *Barnette.* His stance cast him in the opposition, his leadership had been rejected. From Frankfurter's psychological viewpoint, he felt as if he were under siege and had no choice but to remain where he was and fight it out. These circumstances vitally affected his relationships with other Justices and the content of his jurisprudence.

It is at this point that Hirsch's analysis becomes at once most useful and most controversial. Hirsch argues that "the key to Frankfurter's political behavior was his attitude toward opposition." Because Frankfurter's psychological peace rested on an inflated self-image, Frankfurter could not accept serious, sustained opposition in fields he considered his domain of expertise. Projecting his own self-doubt, Frankfurter reacted to his opponents with vindictive hostility. From this premise, Hirsch goes on to claim that the opposition to Frankfurter on the Court pushed Frankfurter "into jurisprudential corners from which he never extricated himself."

What started out for Frankfurter as a tentative nod toward deference became a total commitment and Frankfurter's principal philosophic shield against his opponents. Frankfurter became so intent on beating his adversaries that he became obsessed by an austere doctrine of judicial self-restraint that "choked off the opportunity for a truly creative jurisprudence." For example, Frankfurter's pre-Court commitment to greater judicial scrutiny of laws regulating civil liberties than of those regulating economics gave way, under the psychological press of opposition on the Court, to a hardening of his concept of judicial deference so as to be unwilling to rank constitutional values. Thus does Hirsch launch a sweeping psychological explanation—a psychological Occam's Razor—for the constitutional philosophy of one of the most influential jurists of the twentieth century.

Hirsch's effort at psychobiography is entrancing. It offers an important clue to the contrast between Frankfurter before his Court appointment and Frankfurter after he became a Justice. To some extent, it makes more understandable how a man known as a civil libertarian—and even a radical—became, once on the bench, our most famous and persistent spokesman for austere judicial self-restraint. It suggests a reason for Frankfurter's isolated, embittered, and ineffective tenure on the Court. By turning a searchlight on the darker side of Frankfurter's character, Hirsch finds what he thinks is a plausible explanation for Frankfurter's entire judicial performance. It is a convincing tour de force.

In a larger sense, Hirsch's book raises the problem of applying psychological theory to biography in general and to judicial biography in particular. Aware that such techniques have met only "mixed success," Hirsch thinks "careful psychological analysis of the [Supreme Court's] members is necessary for a full understanding of the workings of the institution." Although he disclaims any attempt to reduce a judge's jurisprudence "to the content of his psyche," it is clear that Hirsch believes we cannot truly comprehend a judge's jurisprudence without at least examining his psyche. But all the same, as Hirsch realizes, psychobiography is not a substitute for traditional ideological analysis, but rather its complement.

"Elegant bunk" is how Justice Frank Murphy dismissed Frankfurter's scholarly opinions. But no one could reasonably use the same phrase to describe Hirsch's admirable first effort in a new genre: judicial psychobiography. Future biographers of Supreme Court Justices will at a minimum have to consider the impact of a subject's psychological life on his legal philosophy. Of course, there is a risk of outlandish or silly analysis. But that risk is offset by the potential gain provided by insight.

19

Earl Warren

Autobiography is a difficult literary genre. The auto-
biographer walks a tightrope between, on the one hand,
obnoxious preoccupation with himself and his own self-importance with respect to exciting historical events, and, on
the other hand, a boring, flat recitation of his life experiences. Perhaps the unavoidable difficulties of the genre explain why autobiography rarely appears in the first rank of
literature. H. L. Mencken's glorious three-volume autobiography qualifies, but others do not spring readily to
mind.

Even so, an autobiography—a rather pedestrian one at
that—can be useful, particularly where the subject has had
an eventful and controversial life.

Earl Warren's life, which ended in 1974, was nothing if
not eventful and controversial. Crusading and incorruptible
District Attorney in Oakland, California; Attorney General
and three-term Governor of California; Chief Justice of the
United States; and chairman of the commission that inves-
tigated President Kennedy's assassination—Earl Warren
was all of these, and more.

Unprivate as Warren's life was, it may still be news to
learn that Warren was the candidate of *both* major parties
in one of his gubernatorial campaigns and that he had

much national political influence while Governor of California. Of course, Warren's memoirs discuss his public life (though his years on the Supreme Court get comparatively, and surprisingly, few pages), but that is not where their usefulness lies.

The major contribution of Warren's autobiography is the insight it gives into understanding and appreciating Earl Warren. Freud is too much with us to discount the shaping quality of early events in one's life, and Warren freely recognizes the strong influence of his youthful experiences among poor railroad workers, with their labor troubles, economic hardships, and generally low position in the social order. Given such experience, do Warren's decisions as Chief Justice come as a surprise?

Consider the *ad hominem* criticism of the author of *Miranda* and the Chief of the Supreme Court that decided other landmark cases recognizing procedural rights of criminal defendants. "Soft on criminals," said the critics. But how many of them knew that Warren understood from first-hand experience what it meant to be a victim of violent crime or a member of the victim's family? That Warren's father was brutally murdered during Warren's first campaign to be State Attorney General? Or that Warren had been a vigorous law enforcement officer as District Attorney and Attorney General, sometimes cross-examining witnesses so forcefully that he later regretted trenching upon their claims of self-incrimination?

With ill-concealed bitterness, Warren recalls Senator Joseph McCarthy saying on the floor of the Senate, "I will not say that Earl Warren is a Communist, but I will say he is the best friend of Communism in the United States." Yet as District Attorney of Alameda County, Earl Warren prosecuted cases under his state's Criminal Syndicalism Act. In 1927 one of Warren's prosecutions wended its way up to the United States Supreme Court in *Whitney* v. *California*, and led to Justice Brandeis's memorable concurring opinion, a magnificent stump speech for democracy and First Amendment freedoms.

Warren could take strong action when he thought national security was genuinely in peril, as shown by his crucial support of the program to relocate Japanese-Americans in California during World War II. He lived to regret giving such support, however, later believing the authorities (including himself) acted too hastily in relocating people simply on the basis of ancestry. "Invidious discrimination," he might say if he were alive today.

But Warren was not alone in his advocacy of the detention of Japanese-Americans because of the wartime exigencies. Justice Hugo Black, that great champion of civil liberties, authored the Supreme Court's opinion in *Korematsu*, upholding the constitutionality of the detention program, but, unlike Warren, never retreated from his position.

Two apparently unconnected events display the inconsistencies and contradictions that show up in Warren's life, just as they probably would in the life of anyone who lives past eighty. As a young district attorney, Warren had no qualms about speaking *ex parte* to the Chief Justice of the California Supreme Court about pending indictments; but later as Chief Justice of the United States he was appalled when Attorney General John Mitchell tried to have *ex parte* communications about pending cases. What happened in the interim to make Chief Justice Warren more sensitive than D.A. Warren? Is it simply the difference between an advocate and a judge? Or perhaps a result of maturity?

Although Warren says that his tenure on the Supreme Court capped his career, in his memoirs he really scants his judicial service. He includes the obligatory references to the cases on school desegregation, reapportionment, and the rights of criminal defendants, but, unfortunately, adds no new information.

The reader who presumably picked up Warren's memoirs for the rare insight they might afford into the workings and personalities of the Supreme Court is disappointed. Warren had a peculiarly advantageous post from which to observe and comment on his colleagues on the Court, but he says nothing—and it is our loss.

Warren emerges as sincere and well-meaning, though perhaps a mite self-righteous and overly serious. The most humorous incident related by Warren is about California's old method of bar examinations: having a judge of the State Supreme Court personally ask the applicant two questions, one correct answer being enough to pass. If the first answer was wrong, the judge would say: "I am sorry, your answer is wrong. Now for the second question. What is the doctrine of cy pres?" If the applicant replied, "I don't know," the judge would announce, "That is correct, you don't; and you have passed the examination."

20

William O. Douglas

AMONG Supreme Court Justices, William O. Douglas is unique. He served the longest, wrote the most opinions, wrote the most books, was the most radical civil libertarian, and had the most wives. But Douglas's true uniqueness cannot be gauged by a crass form of more-is-better— using an easily measured quantity to assess improperly a far more subtle and elusive quality. What made Douglas special was his attitudes, his mountain climbing, his hatred of what he unoriginally called the "powers that be" and the "establishment," his worldwide travels, and his willingness to stand alone. Yet Douglas's real nature remains hidden.

Indeed, there is something curious about the second volume of Douglas's autobiography *(The Court Years)*. What makes the memoirs curious is not what they say, but, like the dog who failed to bark in the Sherlock Holmes tale, what they don't say. Not surprisingly, the autobiography is filled with anecdotes and comments by Douglas on his relationships with other Justices, with Presidents, and on the work of the Supreme Court. But the autobiography totally misses perhaps the most pivotal aspect of Douglas's life by ignoring or failing to recognize both the existence and significance of Douglas's psychological development.

In a recent biography of Douglas entitled *Independent Journey*, Professor James F. Simon of New York Law School is much more sensitive to his subject's psychological development. As he tells Douglas's life story, Professor Simon portrays Douglas's puritanical and poverty-stricken upbringing, his driving ambition, his problem in breaking loose from a dominant mother, and his well-known difficulties with women. Based on these observations, Simon offers occasional insights of great value into particular facets of Douglas's life. But Simon, too, fails to connect Douglas's psychological life to his overall judicial work. If such a connection exists, finding it will give more meaning to Douglas's judicial work and significantly deepen our understanding of the mind that produced such work.

The suggestion here is that Douglas suffered a delayed mid-life crisis that had a profound impact on his judicial work, that clearly divided his jurisprudence into "before" and "after." The diagnosis finds ample supporting evidence in publicly available information, from well-known events in Douglas's personal life, judicial opinions, and nonjudicial writings. Each of these three areas provides telltale signs of a mid-life crisis. Taken together, they make out a case that is unanswerable.

In Douglas's personal life two watershed events—a near-fatal accident and the breakup of his first marriage—occurred at about the same time. In October 1949, at the age of fifty, Douglas fell while horseback riding and, as his horse rolled over him, suffered a crushed chest, twenty-three or twenty-four broken ribs, and a punctured lung. He spent months recuperating, months filled with time to think and reflect on his brush with death and his own mortality.

By the time of his accident, Douglas's marriage to his

first wife was unraveling. Having married young, Douglas was divorced in 1953 after twenty-nine years of marriage. Then followed a series of three marriages to women in their twenties, two of them college students. For anyone with Douglas's strong, religious childhood—his father was a preacher—it would be absurd to deny the psychological importance of divorce, particularly after a marriage of three decades. For a man in his fifties to end a long-term relationship and start new relationships with women thirty years younger than himself is a classic symptom of a mid-life crisis.

At about the time of his divorce, Douglas's judicial opinions started to change. By the end of his tenure on the Court, Douglas's work-product had changed so much that it bore no resemblance to what it was when he first was appointed. These marked changes related to both substance and style.

Before the mid-1950s, Douglas was not the great civil libertarian he became later. With Justices Black, Murphy, and Rutledge also on the Court, Douglas would probably rank no better than fourth as a consistent civil libertarian during the 1940s. After all, Douglas had upheld the exclusion of Japanese-Americans during World War II, and had upheld, over religious objections, a compulsory flag salute when the issue first reached the Court in 1940. In other cases, he upheld the deportation of a former Communist and approved released-time religious training, saying, "We are a religious people whose institution presupposes the existence of a Supreme Being." These were not the cases on which Douglas built his reputation for civil liberties.

Around 1953, all this was transformed. Before that Douglas had been unwilling to abandon Justice Holmes's "clear and present danger" test, though he usually had held that the government had failed to meet its burden. But in 1953—the year of his divorce—Douglas's judicial opinions involving the scope of free expression assumed an absolutist cast. Douglas even went on to extend his absolutist view beyond discussion of public issues to private speech uttered for private purposes. Similarly, it was not until 1952 that Douglas adopted the view that unauthorized governmental wiretapping violated the Fourth Amendment.

Once the turning point had come, there was no looking back for Douglas. In every field of civil liberties—freedom of expression, religion, criminal procedure, privacy, race and sex discrimination—Douglas's opinions grew more and more protective and absolute. He never repeated his conservative decisions of the 1940s. It is hard to imagine the Douglas of the 1960s or '70s, magnificent then in his defense of the individual against society, ever having voted the way he did in certain cases in the mid-1940s.

With the change in substance came a drastic change in style. Anyone with eyes to see can note the extraordinary differences between, say, Douglas's lengthy, careful, clear, and painstaking opinion for the Court in the 1940 *Socony Vacuum* antitrust case, and his later series of stump speeches and collections of aphorisms that often lacked the organization and logical structure of traditional judicial opinions. His opinions, as Simon points out, "often appeared superficial or just plain sloppy. . . . After his first decade on the Court, Douglas appeared to have been interested more in communicating his broad philosophy to the readers of his judicial opinions than in satisfying a scholar's appetite for carefully documented legal arguments."

"When Douglas first came to the Court," said Harvard Professor Paul Freund, "he wrote a little differently. He took more pains with his opinions. In areas such as railroad reorganization, he was quite masterful in getting command of the intricate facts. Later, it seemed to me he showed less interest in painstaking opinions. His opinions seemed written for a general audience. It was as if he got bored with the lawyer's craft."

Even his nonjudicial writings show the same pattern. Before the early 1950s, Douglas's books were travelogues based on his trips abroad, or hymns to nature based on the majesty of the Pacific Northwest. Starting in the early fifties, he wrote more political books that often expanded on his civil libertarian views. These writings culminated in *Points of Rebellion*, a silly ninety-seven-page book published in 1970, which seemed—the arguments were none too clear—to call for revolution. Anyone looking at the development of Douglas's nonjudicial writings must notice a change in subject in the early '50s.

How does one explain the palpable pattern in Douglas's life? Several explanations are possible. Advancing age could have made him impatient with scholarly judicial opinions when he thought it more important to cut through the legal intricacies to get to the basic human problem. Or he may have wanted to become a conscious hero of the young. Possibly he broke through a creative barrier, going through some form of "peak experience" around 1953. However that may be, the mind of the Justice is all but hidden in his two-volume autobiography.

If Douglas is to be truly understood, his delayed mid-life crisis will have to be faced. That crisis—brought about by accumulated psychological tensions, accelerated professional success, an almost fatal accident, and a failed long-term relationship with a woman—seems central to Douglas's style and his vision as a judge. Something snapped in Douglas's psyche in the early 1950s and freed him from much of his past.

When the definitive biography of Douglas comes to be written, it will have to explain how his delayed mid-life crisis shaped his interpretation of constitutional law. Approached from this perspective, the texture of Douglas's life thickens and his biography takes on another order of significance.

21

Justice Stewart's Craft *

IN APPRAISALS of American jurists, attention has focused
on whether a particular judge is a conservative or liberal,
loose or strict constructionist, advocate of judicial restraint
or judicial activism. But there may be an even more basic
factor in judicial decision making at the highest levels that
has escaped attention—a factor that may be called doctrinalism.

There are two poles on the scale of doctrinalism. At one
end, the decision-maker has an overarching philosophy (of
constitutional law, for example) against which he considers
each individual case. On the other end, the jurist approaches each case on an individual basis, without reference to an overall conceptual approach.

Many judges of the first type—the constitutional system-
builders—have become familiar to lawyers and laymen
alike, precisely because they so clearly embody a particular
approach to constitutional issues. Hugo Black, with his absolutist approach to the First Amendment and his incorporation theory of applying the Bill of Rights to the states
via the Fourteenth Amendment, comes readily to mind. So
do William Douglas, Felix Frankfurter, and William
Rehnquist.

* Co-authored with my law partner, Marvin Wexler.

The similarity between these jurists lies not in the particulars of their views on specific issues—which differ markedly—but in the largeness of their ideas. Such comprehensiveness necessarily blurs some distinctions—mere quibbles, these judges might say—occasionally making decision making seem easy and predictable. For example, once a challenged activity qualified as speech, it was no hard task to guess how Black and Douglas would vote.

Such system-builders could assemble their logic into neat and often beguiling syllogisms that gave the impression that they had considered, and resolved to their satisfaction, every facet of every conceivable case that could arise under a particular statutory or constitutional provision.

The second type of judge—the case-by-case jurist—is typified by Potter Stewart. In his twenty-three years on the Court, Stewart wrote hundreds of opinions and took part in thousands of decisions running the full range of federal law. His decisions fit no obvious category and defy easy labels.

The inability to squeeze Stewart's work into pigeonholes makes analysis and evaluation at once more difficult and more intriguing. This difficulty has misled some commentators to conclude recently that Stewart had no overall judicial or constitutional philosophy, and that as a result he left less of an imprint on the law.

The basic error of this conclusion is its assumption that the only frames of reference in evaluating judicial work are shopworn labels that so often beg the question and discourage further inquiry. If a Justice or his work refuses to be so facilely cabined, many commentators are at a loss as to what to do.

His opinions show that Stewart saw his duty as no more

and no less than to decide the particular case presented, not to write a treatise on the law. Stewart had a tight, lean style of opinion-writing, marked by close attention to facts and by narrow holdings limited to such facts. Rarely did he reach beyond the scope of the facts in the case before him to generalize about the state of the law. For this reason, his opinions invariably were much shorter than those of his colleagues.

In his case-by-case approach, Stewart is more faithful than the system-builders to the common law tradition. In that tradition, law emerges inductively by means of case-by-case development. The particular facts of one case produce a rule to be applied in future cases involving like facts, and legal principles are modified or extended by the slow processes of analyzing and distinguishing. The common law tradition thus depended much less on *a priori* system-building than on deciding individual cases that, over time, became a body of law.

This was the way of the great Holmes, among others. Even with his philosophical bent and vast store of learning, Holmes never was much for system-building. His distrust of general propositions led him to approach each case without being hamstrung by concepts and categories. About the only general proposition Holmes acted on as a judge was that legislation should not lightly be overturned or otherwise judicially modified, a proposition that grew out of Holmes's general skepticism and his acquiescence in democratic principles. Apart from this one principle, though, Holmes was solidly on the side of case-by-case analysis, with its sensitivity to subtlety and nuance so often ignored by more doctrinaire approaches.

Holmes's unsystematic performance as a judge has stood the test of time. Contemporary commentators should not underestimate Stewart's contribution to federal law, constitutional and otherwise, just because he professed no "system."

In fact, the system-building approach has inherent weaknesses. Whatever the system, it tends to be mechanical jurisprudence in which definitions lead to foreordained results. That is in the nature of deductive systems. Such slot-machine jurisprudence, even if built on valid theory, is at times too wooden, inflexible and predictable.

Lack of predictability in a judge can be a good quality. The art of judging is careful consideration, weighing and balancing of evidence, legal argument, and other relevant factors in each case. By the time a case wends its way to the Supreme Court, it necessarily involves very significant issues. One hopes that such issues will be evaluated carefully and individually. Consequently, to be called a "swing" Justice, as Stewart often was, may be a high compliment reflecting an unpredictability born of attention to real distinctions not always apparent to systematic criteria.

To be sure, unpredictability or lack of doctrinalism is by itself no virtue. Justices with weak personalities or without strong intellectual equipment may flip-flop back and forth on issues without any discernible reason. A bad judge does not become a good judge by being a straw in the wind. On the other hand, a good judge does not become a bad judge simply because he defies journalistic labels.

In this sense, Stewart's most quotable line—"I know it when I see it"—epitomizes his approach to decisionmaking. Where others might have a tendency to prejudge an issue, bending the case to fit preconceived doctrine, Stewart would look closely at the facts and only then decide the issue presented. In short, where others might not even look, Stewart would take the time and care to see.

A healthy jurisprudence should be large and vibrant enough to sustain more than one style of decision making. There is no reason why system-builders and ad hoc decisionmakers cannot coexist side by side, to overall benefit. Their different styles are not so much in tension as they are in synergy. Perhaps the next generation of system-builders will stand on Justice Stewart's shoulders, relying upon the distinctions he drew as the basis for its own new system.

22

Abe Fortas

Aʙᴇ ꜰᴏʀᴛᴀs, the only Supreme Court justice ever to resign under public criticism, had one of the most interesting and curious legal careers in American history. Even his death in April 1982 was noteworthy. He died only a few weeks after he had made his first oral argument before the Supreme Court since his resignation in 1969. Although he was in private practice for thirteen years after he resigned from the Supreme Court, the tragic truth is that, from the time of his resignation, Fortas ceased to be a significant force in American law. How Fortas came to end up this way is an instructive tale, with lasting lessons.

Fortas's life, considered in perspective, had three major turning points. The first crucial event for Fortas was going to Yale Law School. Next came Fortas's unusually close relationship with a man who became President of the United States. The third and final decisive occurrence was his Supreme Court resignation. These three events—law school, closeness with Lyndon Johnson, and resignation—organize Fortas's life, all seventy-one years of it.

I

The early part of Fortas's career is a tribute to meritocracy and upward mobility in American society. Like many other prominent Americans, Fortas started life obscurely. He was born in Tennessee to immigrant working-class parents, who sent him to local public schools and Southwestern College in Memphis. After college, Fortas left Tennessee for good. We are so accustomed to thinking of Fortas as part of the sophisticated Washington scene that we often ignore his Tennessee roots.

From Tennessee Fortas made the fateful trip north to New Haven, Connecticut, to study law at Yale. Yale has always been a special place to learn law, and never more so than in the early 1930s when Fortas studied there. Drawing outstanding college graduates from across the nation, Yale Law School was—and is—a small sociological and academic filtering system in which students of ability and promise cut their teeth on the rigors of legal analysis. Yale's faculty, which in Fortas's time included such notables as Charles Clark, Arthur Corbin, Thurman Arnold, and Wesley Sturges, has always stressed the social aspects of legal decision making. In the 1920s and 1930s, Yale Law School was the center of a controversial new doctrine called Legal Realism, which tried to cut through the formalism of law to its essence, to its social and economic roots. To this day, Yale Law School has a well-deserved reputation for going beyond technical legal rules to the policy considerations underlying them.

In Yale's atmosphere of scholarly legal ferment, Fortas flourished. He studied hard and did well—so well, in fact, that he was named editor-in-chief of the Yale Law Journal. Then, as now, the Yale Law Journal was one of the most prestigious law reviews in America. To be editor-in-chief of such a prestigious law review is as good a sign as one can get of potential success in the law. It is roughly the equivalent of winning the Heisman Trophy in football, or at least making the All-American Team.

For Fortas, as for others before and since, Yale Law
School was the vehicle of transition from provincial ob-
scurity to the world of law in the grand manner. Following
graduation in June 1933, Fortas planned to stay on as a
junior law teacher. But this was the middle of the Depression and the early New Deal, when many young lawyers
went to Washington to staff new government agencies. Following some of his professors who had migrated South to
the nation's capital, Fortas started a thirteen-year stint of
government service.

After tours of duty at the Agricultural Adjustment Administration and the Securities and Exchange Commission,
Fortas went to the Department of the Interior. By 1942, at
the age of thirty-two, Fortas became Under Secretary of the
Interior, the chief assistant to Harold Ickes, Secretary of the
Interior. In this role Fortas began to exhibit some of the
traits that would later become his hallmark. For example,
he tried, manfully but unsuccessfully, to halt the intern-
ment of persons of Japanese descent on the West Coast.
With more success, he and Ickes were able to soften the
strict martial law that the military had imposed on Hawaii.
These efforts by Fortas on behalf of individual liberties
were harbingers of Fortas's future approach to law.

Leaving the government in 1946, he did what most if not
all lawyers secretly yearn to do: he founded a new law firm.
Fortas joined former assistant attorney general and federal
appeals judge Thurman Arnold to practice law in Washington. Soon afterward former Federal Communications Commissioner Paul Porter came aboard, and the firm of Arnold,
Fortas & Porter was born. The three founders imposed their
own distinctive style on the practice of law. In addition to
corporations, the young law firm represented government
officials and politicians. One of these politicians, an ob-

scure congressman from Texas named Johnson, would greatly alter Fortas's life.

In 1948 Lyndon Johnson was a not very well known congressman from Texas. In that year, he retained Abe Fortas as his attorney in an important election case. The case arose from the Democratic primary for senator from Texas that year, which Johnson won by eighty-seven votes. Johnson's opponent sued in federal court, alleging various voting irregularities. The federal court issued an order to keep Johnson's name off the ballot for the general election. After being retained and having considered the problem, Fortas appealed to Justice Hugo Black, the Circuit Justice for Texas, who reversed the lower court order, thereby allowing Johnson's name back on the ballot. As a result of Fortas's successful legal maneuver, Johnson won the general election and began his career in the Senate. Thereafter he relied heavily on Fortas's counsel.

As the relationship between Fortas and Johnson deepened, the law firm of Arnold, Fortas & Porter grew and prospered. It became one of the leading law firms in Washington, with a full roster of large corporate clients. Still, it was a law firm with a difference. To be sure, it did agency work, litigation, and all the other tasks that full-service Washington law firms do. But its founders had an admirable philosophy of law practice that combined making good with doing good. Fortas and his partners institutionalized *pro bono* cases as part of their practice, with the paying clients in effect subsidizing civil liberties cases that the firm took on for free. During the McCarthy era, Fortas and his partners represented several so-called security risks, most notably Owen Lattimore.

Some of Fortas's most spectacular successes as a lawyer came in cases for which he did not receive a regular fee. In 1954 Fortas served as court-appointed counsel for the defendant in *Durham* v. *United States*, the landmark case in which the United States Court of Appeals for the District of Columbia adopted a new test of criminal insanity. Abandoning the old English *McNaghten* test, the Court of Appeals agreed with Fortas that a person should not be considered responsible for his criminal act if he was suffering, at the time he committed the act, from a mental disease and if the act was a product of that disease. In 1963, the Supreme Court appointed Fortas to represent an indigent who claimed his conviction should be reversed because he had had no lawyer to defend him at trial. In that famous case, *Gideon* v. *Wainwright*, Fortas convinced the Supreme Court to overrule one of its precedents and hold that the Sixth Amendment right to counsel requires the states to provide trial lawyers to all persons accused of serious crimes. To many experts, Fortas's victory in *Gideon* ushered in the "criminal law revolution" by the Supreme Court, a revolution in which Fortas would participate not only from the lawyer's lectern but also from the Justices' bench.

While Johnson was Vice President and President, Fortas continued to be an informal confidential legal adviser. Fortas was the one to whom Johnson turned to organize the Warren Commission and its investigation of the assassination of President Kennedy. After Robert Kennedy resigned as Attorney General in 1964, Johnson offered the job to Fortas, but Fortas turned it down. Then, in July 1965, after Arthur Goldberg left the Supreme Court to become the United States delegate to the United Nations, Johnson appointed Fortas to the Supreme Court. Although Fortas initially protested, ultimately he accepted.

On the Supreme Court, Fortas continued some of the themes seen earlier in his career. His was one of the five votes in favor of *Miranda* v. *Arizona,* and in important cases he voted to hold unconstitutional certain loyalty-security measures. He frequently voted to protect criminal defendants' rights. In one particular area, the constitutional rights of juvenile offenders, Fortas led the way. In his important opinion for the Court in *In re Gault,* he held that juvenile offenders are entitled to many of the constitutional rights required in adult court proceedings. By 1968, Fortas had begun to acquire a reputation as a tough liberal Justice who in the next several years could be expected to become quite influential among his colleagues.

III

But Fortas was not to have several years on the Court. The first hint of trouble came in the summer of 1968 when President Johnson nominated Fortas to succeed the retiring Earl Warren as Chief Justice. Questioned by the Senate Judiciary Committee, Fortas admitted that while a Justice he had participated in White House strategy conferences and had otherwise advised the President. There were even other charges of extra-judicial activities, including the disturbing disclosure that as a Justice Fortas had received a fee of $15,000 (compared to his $39,500 salary) from prominent businessmen for giving a brief university seminar. In October, after the Senate failed to cut off an anti-Fortas filibuster, Fortas asked that his name be withdrawn. Of course, it is impossible to say whether the Senate's opposition was based on Fortas's extra-judicial activities or on Fortas's liberalism. In any event, it boded ill for Fortas.

In May 1969, in an article entitled "The Justice . . . and the Stock Manipulator," *Life* magazine reported that after going on the bench, Fortas had received a $20,000 fee from the family foundation of Louis E. Wolfson, who had since been imprisoned for federal securities violations. The article pointed out that Fortas gave back the fee eleven months later, after Wolfson had been twice indicted. Although the story admitted that there was no evidence "making possible a charge that Wolfson had hired Fortas to fix his case," it went on to say that "Justice Fortas's name was being dropped in strategic places" by Wolfson.

On the day the article appeared, Fortas issued an unsatisfying statement. On the one hand, Fortas denied accepting "any fee or emolument from Mr. Wolfson or the Wolfson Family Foundation or any related person or group." On the other hand, Fortas did admit that in 1966 the Wolfson Family Foundation had "tendered" a fee to him for research services, but that he later returned the fee. Two days later, Attorney General John Mitchell met with Chief Justice Warren for the purpose, according to *Newsweek*, of informing him that the Justice Department had "far more serious" information than had been revealed, and that it would be best for the Court if Fortas could be persuaded to resign. Meanwhile, there was talk in Congress of impeaching Fortas.

Nine days after the original *Life* article, Fortas resigned. In a long letter to Chief Justice Warren explaining his resignation, Fortas made even further disclosures. In addition to the $20,000 fee that he received and paid back, Fortas had contracted with the Wolfson Foundation to receive $20,000 a year for life and for the life of his wife if she outlived him. Fortas also admitted in the letter that at times Wolfson did bring up his legal problems to Fortas. Protesting that "there has been no wrongdoing on my part," Fortas said he was resigning for the good of the Court.

So it was that after only four years as a Supreme Court

Justice, Fortas reentered private practice. But his second career as a practicing lawyer was anticlimatic. He did not return to the law firm he had founded. Instead he and another lawyer started a small firm in Washington, lobbying, litigating, and rendering legal advice. As time passed, Fortas saw many of his judicial opinions eroded by the Burger Court. All in all, his post-Court years could not have been happy ones.

There are disturbing parallels between Abe Fortas and Richard Nixon. Both men fell in disgrace from pinnacles of power for basically stupid and unnecessary decisions. Both men apparently did not see that what they were doing was wrong. Both men were condemned to live out their remaining years thinking about what might have been. Most distressing of all, both men acted at times as if they were above the law.

In the case of Fortas, his behavior is particularly hard to explain. Cupidity cannot be the explanation. Surely Fortas did not need Wolfson's money, not after twenty years as one of the most prominent lawyers in Washington and not while his wife was still a senior tax partner at Arnold & Porter. Nor can anyone accuse Fortas of being stupid or foolish, not after a professional lifetime built on a reputation for shrewd and astute judgment. No, the true explanation lies elsewhere.

Perhaps the real explanation is the unfortunate feeling of some of the powerful that they need not abide by the same rules as everyone else. Fortas at times acted as if he had his own code of conduct, without regard to other peoples' opinions. For example, Fortas never expressed any misgivings about his extra-judicial activities. And yet the very thought of a sitting Justice drafting legislation or advising on conduct that may come up for judicial review is fraught with risk for the doctrine of separation of powers. As the true depth of such extrajudicial conduct by Fortas and other Justices (e.g., Brandeis and Frankfurter) becomes known, public reaction grows worse, and with reason. Undoubtedly the post-Watergate environment has made everyone more careful, including Supreme Court Justices.

23

Fred Rodell's Swan Song

FATE turned Fred Rodell's second book into his swan song. Rodell, a maverick Yale law professor who foreswore footnotes early on, wrote *Woe Unto You, Lawyers* in 1939 at the age of thirty-two. He died in 1980, in the same year that his classic was reissued in paperback. Among books about law by American authors, there are only a handful that rest solidly on the shelf. *Woe Unto You, Lawyers* is one of those books. It is funny, it is wise, it goes right on selling, year after year, and with good reason.

For decades Rodell tried to make his law students learn how to write simply and clearly about the law. Unlike some academics, he believed that clear writing reflected clear thinking and that even the most complex legal concepts can be explained intelligibly if the writer truly understands them. Rodell's own works, from books on the Supreme Court to magazine articles, are models of clear and deceptively simple writing about complex and important subjects.

Clarity and simplicity went hand in hand with Rodell's other passions: truth and individual liberties. Rodell tilted with pomposity and fakery wherever he found them, in ordinary law practice and in Supreme Court opinions. He thought courts should use whatever power they could to

right wrongs and strengthen civil liberties. Felix Frankfurter was not one of Rodell's heroes; William O. Douglas
was.

All of these lifelong themes can be found in Rodell's second book. The 1980 edition of *Woe Unto You, Lawyers* is
dedicated, "for the man who, forty-one years ago, gave me
the title for this book—great Justice, great guy, and great
friend—Bill Douglas." Time has not only failed to reduce
the book's importance, but, to the contrary, has made it
more relevant than ever. In memorable prose, the first sentences of the first chapter continue to haunt us: "In tribal
times, there were the medicine men. In the middle ages,
there were the priests. Today, there are the lawyers."

Now, as in 1939, lawyers are divided into two main
camps: those who concentrate on the means, the entan-
gling trappings of the law and its sometimes arcane language; and those who focus on the end, the intelligent,
practical, and socially useful solution of human problems.
Once such a practical solution is found, it can of course be
packaged in respectable legal clothes. But the emphasis, according to Rodell, should be on the end, not the means.

And it is clear from the tenor and style of Rodell's prose
when discussing such potentiality that Rodell is at heart an
optimist with lots of hope, despite his and the book's reputation for debunking. The debunking is merely Rodell's
way of contrasting what *is* with what *should be.*

Some of Rodell's potshots seem at times a bit overdrawn,
as if intended to overstate his case on purpose. Like a good
negotiator, Rodell asks for more than he knows the reader
will agree to, in the hope that the reader ultimately will
concede more than otherwise. Is it really true that the "alleged logic" of any Supreme Court case is "an intellectual
fraud"? A harsh verdict, and unfair, yet it reflects a frank
view of law. Rodell scorned the vague, the tame, the color-

less. His writing had bite to it; it was clear, brief, and bold.

Even today, Rodell's words give anyone interested in law much to reflect on. Rodell is uncomfortable—a regular hairshirt of a man. But his ideas show a profound understanding of the tensions inherent in the law. He is aware of the play of principle and counterprinciple and of the practical considerations that supply the major themes of the law.

His famous book can be reread with undiminished excitement. It stands. It will beckon as long as this remarkable book stays in print—which should be as long as there are lawyers, as long as there are courts. It is ironic to sit here in a busy law office, and hear across more than forty years of time, his diatribes, his overblown criticisms, and his seductive summons to the wildest revel of them all—to do away with all lawyers.

24

Military Law

MILITARY law is a lot like everyday family law. When a small child does something wrong, no parent reads the wee culprit *Miranda* rights, offers him a free lawyer, or tries the scamp by a jury composed of twelve fellow scamps. Rather, justice, in the form of a scold or a slap astern, is meted out on the spot, and that ends the matter. Military law has the same goal and method: discipline by means of punishment swift and certain.

Joseph W. Bishop takes this goal and method as given in his study of military law, *Justice Under Fire*. Bishop teaches torts and corporations as well as military law at Yale, and is a refreshing contrast to misguided academics who think obfuscation is a badge of brilliance. *Justice Under Fire* lives up to his reputation for ability to translate technical legal concepts into simple, readily understandable terms.

With a breezy style that combines earthy side comments with uncommon erudition, Bishop probes all aspects of military law, covering the mechanics and historical background of courts-martial, as well as the war powers, martial law, and war crimes. Unquestionably, Bishop fulfills his hope of writing a "readable" book.

Being "readable," *Justice Under Fire* has an explicit

theme: to show that "contrary to public impression, it [i.e., military law] does have virtues as well as vices." Bishop offers his book as an antidote to such "worthless works," as Robert Sherrill's strident but equally readable book, *Military Justice Is to Justice As Military Music Is to Music.*

To support his point, Bishop notes the procedural advantages enjoyed by an accused in a court-martial. A military defendant, in contrast to a civilian defendant, knows before trial the entire case against him as a result of the investigation required by Article 32 of the Uniform Code of Military Justice. Although the Supreme Court has ruled that statements taken in violation of *Miranda* can be used to impeach a defendant in a civilian trial, courts-martial exclude such statements for *all* purposes. Similarly, the Supreme Court has ruled that no *Miranda* warnings need be given to a civilian suspect asked to provide a handwriting sample, yet such warnings are required before such samples will be admissible in a court-martial.

Bishop's stress on such advantages, however, betokens a lack of a sense of reality. The Constitution of the Soviet Union guarantees civil liberties, but we all know how much dissident thought is actually tolerated there. Similarly, Bishop may cite procedural advantage after advantage, but he is not likely to convince the average enlisted man that courts-martial bend over backwards to deal fairly with servicemen charged with purely military offenses.

If I were a serviceman charged with a purely civilian-type offense, say murder, rape or robbery—I think I would rather be tried by a court-martial than a civilian court, especially in view of local civilian prejudice against servicemen. But a purely military offense, disobedience of an order or disrespect toward a superior, would be an entirely different matter.

It was my experience as an Army legal clerk during the

Vietnam War that no list of paper rights, no matter how long, noble, or advantageous, would present much of an obstacle course to a court-martial bent on punishing a purely military offense. Maybe this is as it should be, given the threat to military society that such offenses pose. In any event, Professor Bishop was a JAG officer, not an enlisted man, in World War II, and perhaps to understand military justice one must see it from the bottom up.

Bishop's lack of feeling for the realities of military life shows up clearly in his treatment of the general military articles. Those articles prohibit "conduct unbecoming an officer and a gentleman," "conduct prejudicial to good order and discipline," and "conduct of a nature to bring discredit upon the armed forces." Bishop says that in "actual practice, the articles are not so vague as they look," and implies that they are not void for vagueness because servicemen tried under them know ahead of time that what they did was wrong, even if not expressly proscribed.

But he totally ignores the two other basic values protected by the void-for-vagueness doctrine: prevention of arbitrary decisions by enforcement authorities and solicitude for constitutionally protected conduct swept within an overly broad statute. Bishop's views were cited by Justice Blackmun, concurring in the Supreme Court's 5-to-3 decision in 1974 in *Parker* v. *Levy*, upholding the constitutionality of the General Articles. But nothing in Justice Rehnquist's majority opinion adequately answers Justice Stewart's comment in dissent:

"The question before us is not whether the military may adopt substantive rules different from those that govern civilian society, but whether the serviceman has the same right as his civilian counterparts to be informed as to precisely what conduct those rules prescribe before he can be criminally punished for violating them."

Because they are unnecessary, Bishop favors repealing the General Articles and replacing them with specific punitive provisions.

Bishop accurately points out that, prior to *Levy*, the Court of Military Appeals and lower federal courts had often said that servicemen retain all constitutional rights except those expressly or impliedly withdrawn. An express exception, like the grand jury exception in the Fifth Amendment, is easy to identify; implied exceptions, by their nature, are more open to debate. But implied exceptions must be based on more than mere incantations of the magic words "military necessity" or "discipline." Someone must examine the relationship between applying a particular constitutional right and its practical effect on military discipline.

Professor Bishop, unfortunately, has little that is original to add to this discussion. To be sure, he says that "military justice should have no greater scope than is absolutely required to maintain military discipline." Yet, in the teeth of every basic canon of statutory construction, he accepts the conventional wisdom that the explicit military exception in the Fifth Amendment does not mean that the other Bill of Rights apply to servicemen. Nor does he even begin to doubt the constitutionality of giving an enlisted man no more than one-third enlisted men on a court-martial panel, while an officer gets an all-officer panel.

My company at Fort Hood, Texas had an average educational level of three years of college, including Ph.D's, architects, writers, and lawyers. Could Bishop or anyone else pretend that a court-martial panel composed of such servicemen would be less able than a panel manned by officers like Lieutenant Calley?

In the last analysis, Professor Bishop's book is an entertaining disappointment. It is a lively compendium of military law, rich in historical background and common sense. Regrettably, his learning and wit were not enlisted in a campaign to find novel and creative approaches to tough problems. Yet, if *Justice Under Fire* keeps alive debate on military law reform—an issue that tends to subside once a war ends—it will for that reason alone deserve a medal.

25

War Crimes

The first lift of C Company touched down at 0730 hours.

Perhaps now, in the sober afterglow of the Vietnam War, we can better consider the implications of this country's attitudes toward war crimes. Those implications go beyond any crimes committed by American troops during that conflict; they extend to basic notions of law and lawlessness. A fascinating study of those implications is contained in *The My Lai Massacre and Its Cover-Up: Beyond the Reach of Law?*, edited by Joseph Goldstein, Burke Marshall, and Jack Schwartz.

As the 1st Platoon moved into the hamlet, its soldiers began placing heavy fire on fleeing Vietnamese, throwing grenades into houses and bunkers.

The book is divided into three main sections. The largest part of the book is the text of Volume I of the official Army investigation of the My Lai incident, also known as "The Peers Report." Even though "The Peers Report" contains little that is new, and despite its restrained and understated official language, the horror of My Lai emerges unmistakably. As the italicized portions of this chapter show, nothing less than a disgusting massacre occurred at My Lai. "The Peers Report" describes the massacre, its origin, and its aftermath—including all attempts to keep it from becoming public.

> *Members of the 2d Platoon began killing Vietnamese inhabi-*
> *tants of My Lai (4) as soon as they entered its western edge . . .*
> *As they advanced and discovered homemade bunkers or bomb*
> *shelters, many of the soldiers yelled "Lai Day" (the Vietnamese*
> *words for "come here"). Failing any response from the Viet-*
> *namese inside the bunkers, the soldiers tossed fragmentation gre-*
> *nades into the bunkers, and followed up by spraying the inside*
> *with small armsfire . . . [W]hen Vietnamese did respond most of*
> *them were shot down as they exited the bunkers.*

Following the text of "The Peers Report," the editors have included a supplement containing various text readings on war crimes from World War II, Nuremberg, and the Vietnam War. These readings are intrinsically interesting, particularly the Supreme Court's decision in the case of General Yamashita, the Japanese commander in the Philippines at the time of the American victory in 1945.

> *Women and children, many of whom were small babies, were*
> *killed sitting or hiding inside their homes. At least two rapes*
> *were participated in and observed by members of the [2d] pla-*
> *toon.*

Yamashita was convicted of war crimes and sentenced to be hanged, not because he participated or even knew about atrocities committed by his troops, but because he allegedly failed as commander to control the operations of his troops, permitting them to commit atrocities. Although the Supreme Court affirmed the conviction and the sentence, it did so over the ringing and prescient dissent of Justice Frank Murphy, which noted that, "The recorded annals of warfare and the established principles of international law afford not the slightest precedent for the charge," and added, "Indeed, the fate of some future President of the United States and his chiefs of staff and military advisers may well have been sealed by this decision."

[A]t least 50 and perhaps as many as 100 inhabitants, comprised almost exclusively of old men, women, children, and babies, were killed by members of one 2d Platoon while they were at My Lai.

In addition to "The Peers Report" and the other original texts, the editors have written an introductory essay entitled, "The Limits of Law: On Establishing Civilian Responsibility for the Enforcement of Laws Against War Crimes." It is the only part of the book written by the editors and, in spite of good intentions, is seriously flawed.

The 1st Platoon's actions in the southwestern portion of My Lai (4) were characterized by one notable, albeit transient, difference from the actions of the 2d Platoon—live detainees were rounded up.

One basic defect in the editors' analysis is their premise that the American military is unable or unwilling to prevent, uncover, or punish war crimes. But the editors themselves prove the contrary. They undercut their premise by publishing "The Peers Report," which describes such crimes in detail and reflects a serious institutional effort to deal with the problem in a forthright way. "The Peers Report" contrasts sharply with the Executive Branch's investigation of Watergate prior to appointment of a special outside prosecutor.

The first group consisted of 60-70 people, comprised primarily of women and children. A few elderly males were also among the group. After reaching the southern edge of the hamlet, the first group was escorted by a few soldiers from the 1st Squad to a ditch.

Nor are the editors entirely fair in blaming the military

for the number of convictions resulting from My Lai. For proof, they point out that Lieutenant Calley was the only person "held to account through the system of military justice," and that several others court-martialed by the Army were acquitted. "This record," say the editors, "cannot be explained by the difficulties of litigation, or the technical problem of courtroom constraints on admissible evidence, or essential weaknesses in the prosecutor's case. It must reflect underlying flaws in the system of accountability that have yet to be identified and understood inside the military or from outside."

. . . A second group of villagers, numbering between 20 and 50, also was moved south . . . and then moved out into the rice paddies where they were placed under guard.

But the editors betray a shocking and studied ignorance of the facts surrounding the war crimes prosecutions during the Vietnam Era. Several American soldiers were court-martialed and convicted in unpublicized incidents. Once individuals were charged in connection with My Lai, the military did not intentionally try to impede the prosecutions. Rather the My Lai prosecutors were given a free hand in preparing and trying their cases, being supplied with whatever logistical support they needed. The My Lai prosecutions were unhampered by command interference, so far as I was aware as special assistant to the prosecution of one of the My Lai defendants. One culprit for the low conviction record may have been Congress, not the military.

Between 0845-0900 hours, the group of villagers (20-50) who had been moved by the 1st Platoon to the south of the hamlet and held under guard in the rice paddies were shot down by members of the platoon.

Congress refused to allow defense counsel to inspect pre-trial testimony given to a congressional subcommittee by prospective government witnesses. As a result, the military judge in at least one case precluded the prosecution from calling those witnesses, and thus contributed to the verdict of not guilty. Yet Congress somehow escapes criticism by the editors. Perhaps even more puzzling, portions of Calley's court opinions reprinted in the volume deal with Congress's conduct, so that the reader wonders at the editors' conclusion. It is ironic for the editors to propose to correct the military's indifference to war crimes by a study through, of all things, a congressional committee.

At approximately 0900-0915 hours, Vietnamese personnel who had been herded into the ditch were shot down by members of the 1st Platoon.

Another stubborn fact completely overlooked by the editors in their wholesale attack on military training is that some soldiers at My Lai refused to obey orders to kill noncombatants. Why did some soldiers obey and others disobey illegal orders? The training may be adequate; it may be the caliber of soldier that is not.

[B]y the time C Company was prepared to depart the area, its members had killed no less than 175-200 Vietnamese men, women and children.

Finally, the specific cure advanced by the editors—trial of war crimes in the District Court for the District of Columbia—would require juries of civilians, whereas military tribunals can offer juries composed of combat veterans with a better understanding of the actual conditions under which the alleged offense occurred. Isn't that what a trial by jury of one's "peers" means?

There is no substantive evidence to indicate that the company received any enemy fire or any other forms of resistance during its movement through the area.

26

Legal Humor

I⊤ is always a joy to read something that punctures the balloon of pomposity, pokes the top hat off phoney respectability, makes us laugh. Humor helps us tackle the day's tasks, whatever they may be.

Jacob A. Stein, who represented a defendant in the Watergate trials, has culled from his humorous columns in *Case and Comment* and elsewhere the selections in his book *Legal Spectator*. He uses two classic ingredients in his humorous mix: surprise and brevity.

Surprise—the unexpected twist, the contrapuntal effect—shows up in almost all of Stein's selections. He adapts O. Henry's short story style to the law, looking at the commonplace from an uncommon point of view.

One of the best selections is Stein's list of "law books which are reached for but absent from the shelf," among them, "The Complete Unwritten Law, in Five Volumes"; "Oral Contracts by Sam Goldwyn (An Oral Contract Ain't Worth the Paper It's Written On)"; and "A Complete Collection of Cases On All Fours." On the same shelf should be Stein's "subtly strange" used volume of F.2d, filled with fake cases deciding issues that have not yet been decided.

He begins another piece by discussing his career as a trial lawyer, adding: "It would seem self-evident that those who are to be designated as Trial Lawyers should take pleasure in trying lawsuits. I am ready to confess that I do not. My pleasure is derived from continuing cases just before trial."

One gem opens with a glorious paragraph about the "pure drama of the courtroom"; follows with the question, "Who could fail to respond with all his attention to the fascination of this spectacle?" and then is devoted to jurors who sleep during trials.

Brevity enhances Stein's efforts. Each selection is short; most run two pages, none more than four. He has mastered the trick of setting up the counterpoint of surprise quickly, and then running. It works.

In his own way, Stein raises and answers an important question: Is it a paradox that humor is the only test of gravity, and gravity of humor? Not really. A subject that cannot be smiled at is suspicious, and a jest that cannot bear serious examination is shallow wit.

Lawyering is surely a subject that can be smiled at, and Stein's smile often becomes a broad and refreshing grin that sometimes even breaks into a hearty bellylaugh. It is hard to keep a straight face when reading that the distinction between man and other forms of animal life is that "man is the only animal who litigates."

Elsewhere, Stein asks why many cases start with great threshold activity but then suddenly stop. "The answer," he says, "is found in the pleading to be known as Notice Under Rule 1. It is filed by the lawyer representing the slow-pay client to alert others that, for the time being at least, the proximate cause of the eclipse is a matter which cannot be attributed to the lack of energy, skill or determination of counsel; and furthermore as soon as the party litigant regains his financial stamina the battle will be renewed *a fortiori cum la forza del dinero.*"

Those of us who draft or respond to interrogatories will

wear a special, knowing smile when we come across this passage: "How I love to receive a set of them. With a connoisseur's eye I compare them to the form interrogatories in my swollen collection. Most sets that come my way are unimaginative copies of one of the six or more master sets produced in the 1950s by those craftsmen who flourished briefly during that golden period of interrogatory framers."

The temptation to give more examples is great. To quote Stein's good lines is to string pearls.

Beneath each of his gibes at lawyering is a serious vein waiting to be mined. Stein knows, just as George Bernard Shaw knew, that satire is a most telling way to make a serious point.

Take, for example, his comment that, "I have learned from experience that no matter how strange and fantastic is my own notion of the law, it is safe to assume that somewhere in the reports there will be a decision that will support it." At once this comment is funny and true, revealing in a subtle fashion the lifeblood of the common law: the dynamic tension between principle and counter-principle.

Lawyers are not the only people continually under an obligation to do things. But they can well appreciate Stein's insight about getting things done: "Oftentimes one finds that he cannot, for some reason, do the job that must be done. One would rather work diligently on something that is irrelevant and unrequired."

27

The Other Holmes

Supreme Court opinions often invoke the legendary name of Holmes. After all, Oliver Wendell Holmes, Jr. is a towering figure in American law—an extraordinary personality, an original scholar, a great judge—and his words still carry weight. But some recent Supreme Court opinions may have started a new trend by citing the work of another Holmes.

The other Holmes is also legendary. Not exactly a lawyer, he nonetheless built his reputation in criminal law. He was, to boot, a contemporary of our Justice Holmes, in a manner of speaking.

Noted for his powers of deduction, the other Holmes probably would have enjoyed a good talk with the Justice about whether the life of the law depended more on logic or experience.

The "other" Holmes is, of course, Sherlock Holmes.

Twice in 1980, Justices of our Supreme Court cited the fictional detective's famous comment about the significance of a dog's failure to bark. In "Silver Blaze," Arthur Conan Doyle has Holmes and Doctor Watson investigate a farm where mysterious things have happened. A police inspector and Holmes have the following exchange:

"'Is there any point to which you would wish to draw my attention?'

"'To the curious incident of the dog in the night-time.'

"'The dog did nothing in the night-time.'

"'That was the curious incident,' remarked Sherlock Holmes."

References to "Silver Blaze" turned up in 1980 Supreme Court opinions dealing with rights of criminal defendants and interpretation of legislative intent.

In one case, the High Court held that a criminal defendant's testimony in his own behalf may be impeached by his prearrest silence. Justice John Paul Stevens concurred with the Court's majority and disagreed with the minority's "assumption that a holding that evidence of silence is admissible necessarily rests on the premise that a quiet person has any duty to speak. . . . A dog's failure to bark may be probative whether or not he has been trained as a watchdog. Cf. A. Conan Doyle, "Silver Blaze," in The Complete Sherlock Holmes (1938)."

In the other case, the Court had to interpret various provisions of the federal Clean Air Act. The first sentence in Justice William Rehnquist's dissent was: "The effort to determine congressional intent here might better be entrusted to a detective than to a judge." Referring to certain legislative action, Rehnquist said it was "no less curious than was the incident in 'Silver Blaze' of the dog that did nothing in the nighttime."

Whatever such judicial opinions may be as law, they surely make for interesting and lively reading. The literary references actually advance the legal arguments.

Citations in Supreme Court opinions to literature are, if not exactly unheard of, at least uncommon. To be sure, dissenters often try to paint a majority's description of the facts as pure fiction, but that's another matter. The number of literary references in nonobscenity cases remains small.

One notable exception was a footnote in a 1974 dissent

by Justice Potter Stewart in which he quoted from Joseph Heller's *Catch-22* to ridicule a majority opinion upholding the constitutionality of vague military laws. In a 1948 case approving the use of public funds for religious-school bussing, Justice Robert Jackson thought the majority's comments about maintaining a wall between church and state were like Byron's Julia who, saying "she would ne'er consent, consented."

Scholars comb Supreme Court opinions for hints of new trends. If the recent references to Sherlock Holmes signal a new style of opinion writing, it is fascinating to imagine what lawyers and judges could do with the literary materials waiting to be mined. For example:

In a decision overruling the *Miranda* warnings, the Court could cite Dostoevsky's *Crime and Punishment* to show that police interrogation stimulates a guilty person's psychological need to confess.

The Hunchback of Notre Dame could figure in a case involving discrimination against the handicapped.

Perhaps *Jane Eyre* could justify allowing people to keep their "crazy" relatives locked up in an attic.

Or *Anna Karenina, Madame Bovary,* and *Sister Carrie* might appear in cases dealing with women's rights.

None of this is meant to disparage the use of literary references in judicial opinions. A prime purpose of a judicial opinion is to persuade, and successful persuasion requires marshalling *all* helpful materials. If literature supplies a dramatic example for demonstrating a legal point, lawyers and judges should use it without reluctance or remorse.

Literature allows us to pick up experience from art, to discover something about other people and ourselves. Law leavened by literature is law closer to life. We should be grateful that our judges read other things besides lawbooks.

28

Race, Sex, and the Law Review

So it finally happened. The Harvard Law Review has decided to take race and sex into account in choosing new editors. But now that affirmative action programs are widespread in our society, why has the Harvard Law Review's decision caused such a stir?

The answer lies in the symbolism of the law review.

Law reviews in America are unique. In no other learned profession or academic discipline are the most prestigious periodicals edited and put out entirely by students. The legal profession looks to these student-run journals for new ideas, theories, syntheses and analyses of legal subjects, and has come to expect the highest quality.

In the past, law review membership was based solely on grades. It was entirely democratic in the sense that distinctions were drawn from allegedly objective intellectual criteria, without regard for one's family background, wealth, or any other irrelevant factor. The farm boy who went to a midwest state university, the slum kid who attended a city college, the preppie who graduated from an Ivy League college—they all could compete for law review and be judged by their merits. It was an admirable concept and embodied strong notions of meritocracy and upward mobility.

But the traditional method of selection had fundamental

flaws. It was an honor society system of double-counting whereby the highest grades—noteworthy achievements in themselves—automatically led to another achievement, law review membership. It also blurred the ultimate purpose of law review because good exam takers do not *necessarily* make the best law review editors.

Amid the student unrest of the late 1960s and early '70s, some law reviews started to change their selection processes. They supplemented grades or replaced them entirely with writing competitions. At Yale, anyone who wanted to, regardless of grades, could join the law review so long as he or she submitted a piece of legal writing judged acceptable by the editors.

Some critics of Harvard's proposed affirmative action plan have suggested that in the future potential employers might discount law review membership. But law review membership should have value aside from its guarantee of a good job. Someone should want to be on law review, not only for its prestige, but for its intrinsic worth.

Law review is intrinsically worthwhile. It teaches discipline, analytic skills, attitudes, and breadth of outlook. It hones one's writing, and a lawyer's primary weapon is wielding the written word. There is a genuine afterglow from publishing a sound law review article that may figure in future cases, briefs, or debates, that may even affect the course of legal thinking. It is not unheard of for student articles to be cited by the Supreme Court.

Law review has a lofty purpose. It should be the cutting edge of the profession. The ideal law review editor should have, in addition to an elephantine appetite for work, a driving desire to think and write about the law. No one should try out for law review unless he or she really likes, even loves, to do that kind of work.

And work there is aplenty on law review. Between read-

ing, writing, and editing legal articles, researching and dou-
ble-checking other authors' research, studying new court
decisions for incipient trends—a law review editor can
easily spend seventy hours a week on top of normal class
time and preparation. There are always more things to do
than time to do them in. Many law students might like to
say they are on law review, but how many are willing to
put in the time and effort demanded?

This reality explodes another criticism of the proposed
Harvard plan: That it makes little sense to compensate for
past disadvantages when choosing "the best among the
best." Many students who gain entry to the nation's most
competitive law schools have the intellectual ability to do
law review work. The question is whether they have the
desire, drive, and energy.

The debate over the Harvard Law Review affirmative action plan seems to miss the basic point of ascertaining the
most relevant criteria for law review membership. Race
and sex do not appear to be nearly as significant in that
regard as ability, creativity, and willingness to do law review work.

The main argument seems to be that law reviews should
not be exempt from general principles governing society,
and that since affirmative action is appropriate elsewhere,
then it should also govern law review selection. Perhaps
the controversy about law review selection says a lot about
the ultimate worth of affirmative action generally and the
hypocrisy of lawyers. Lawyers, themselves largely responsible for affirmative action plans in our society, appear to be
more skeptical of the benefits of such plans in their own
institutions. Is it a case of whose ox is gored?

But the crucial—and unanswerable—point is that race
and sex (and for that matter, wealth, family background,

height, weight, eye or hair color, beauty, and many other attributes) are irrelevant to one's fitness to edit a law review. If we were talking about an athletic team, for example, instead of law review, there would surely be no controversy. Is there a soul so silly as to contend that a college basketball team or football team should take into account anything other than a player's ability, skill, drive, and energy in playing his sport? It is not that athletic teams are exempt from general societal principles; it is just that they vividly illustrate the limited application of what were thought to be general principles. The aim of the venture determines the relevant principles.

The aim of law reviews is to produce the highest quality and most important legal writing possible. In reducing the significance of grades, and laying greater stress on the ability to write and edit a good law review article, the nation's law reviews have over the past decade or so made great strides in the right direction. The whole thrust of that movement has been to identify those characteristics truly bearing on one's performance as a law review editor. The progress made by that movement will be jeopardized by affirmative action, notwithstanding the noble motives and sincerity of the advocates of affirmative action.

Once law reviews pass through their identity crisis, and move away from the traditional view of themselves as honor societies, they will be better able to focus on the crucial task before them. That task is to be the prime source of new and imaginative legal thinking and writing. Seen against the magnitude of that task, quibbling over the place of affirmative action in law review selection shrinks in significance, while at the same time it saps energy and thought away from larger duties.

29

Judge's Dilemma

WHAT should a lower-court judge do if he disagrees with a relevant Supreme Court decision? The Supreme Court itself recently addressed that basic question.

In *Hutto* v. *Davis*, decided in January 1982, the Court summarily reversed a decision by the Fourth Circuit granting a habeas corpus petition challenging a forty-year state prison sentence for possession of less than nine ounces of marijuana as cruel and unusual punishment as proscribed in the Eighth and Fourteenth Amendments. Without benefit of oral argument or full briefing on the merits, but simply on the basis of the certiorari papers, a majority of the Court ruled that the outcome of the case was covered by a recent precedent, *Rummel* v. *Estelle*. In *Rummel*, the Court had rejected an Eighth Amendment argument where a state court had, under a state recidivist statute, sentenced to life imprisonment a defendant on his third felony conviction: obtaining $120.75 by false pretenses.

At the end of its recent *per curiam* decision in *Hutto* v. *Davis*, the Supreme Court said the Fourth Circuit "could be viewed as having ignored, consciously or unconsciously, the hierarchy of the federal court system created by the Constitution and Congress." Using even stronger language, the Court continued: "But unless we wish anarchy to prevail within the federal judicial system, a precedent of this Court must be followed by the lower federal courts no matter how misguided the judges of those courts may think it to be."

Hutto v. *Davis* is an interesting decision in several respects. In terms of procedure, it represents an unusual example of the Court's power to dispose of cases summarily. The unusual summary disposition is even more puzzling in light of the substance of the holding. For, as three Justices pointed out in dissent, it is not at all clear that *Rummel* should control the outcome of *Hutto*. Whereas *Rummel* involved a habitual offender statute, *Hutto* did not. The dissenters in *Hutto* therefore thought the summary procedure was inappropriately employed to change or extend the law in significant ways.

But quite apart from these interesting procedural and substantive issues, it is the Court's sharp warning about anarchy that brings into focus the problems faced by a lower-court judge asked to apply a disagreeable Supreme Court precedent.

What choices has such a lower-court judge?

Follow. The simplest response is to follow the precedent regardless of disagreement. Certainly this is what the Supreme Court thinks is appropriate. But sometimes it can be hard to do so without violating deeply held beliefs.

Most judges have certain bedrock beliefs relating to law, beliefs that may be nonnegotiable. For example, if a judge thinks, like Justices Hugo Black and William Douglas, that the First Amendment is an absolute and that obscenity is protected freedom of speech, must such a judge—*can* such a judge—overcome his constitutional faith and send someone to prison for violating a pornography law? Or suppose a judge agrees with Justices William Brennan and Thurgood Marshall that the death penalty is under all circumstances "cruel and unusual punishment." To ask such a judge to put his imprimatur on a death sentence is asking a lot, even of a seasoned and mature jurist.

But there are choices besides woodenly applying a Supreme Court precedent that a judge thinks is wrong.

Distinguish. A lower-court judge may be able to distinguish a precedent in some principled way. Distinguishing cases comes as easily to judges (or any lawyer for that matter) as running comes to thoroughbreds. We are trained and accustomed to find distinctions.

But there are different kinds of distinctions. Intellectual honesty demands that distinctions be real and principled, not the proverbial distinction without a difference. If a genuine distinction can be found, then the lower-court judge has a possible solution, without violating his personal jurisprudence.

The problem with distinguishing Supreme Court precedents is that the process leaves those precedents intact and uncriticized. Distinguishing creates no dialogue, no process of communication, no debate between lower courts and Supreme Court. The judge, moreover, may reluctantly come to realize that a distinction is impossible and that the obnoxious precedent must cover the case at hand. Even so, there are ways to create a dialogue.

Follow but disagree. If no legitimate distinction exists, one way to keep debate alive is for a lower-court judge to follow and apply the obnoxious precedent, but note disagreement with it and spell out the reasons why the higher court should overrule itself. At the least, this opinion alerts other judges to the problem and represents an appeal to the future, without disrupting the rule of law.

Refuse to follow. An extreme response would be for the lower court to concede the applicability of the precedent, but explicitly refuse to adhere to it. The trouble here is that

Supreme Court precedents are supposed to be overruled only by the Supreme Court, not by lower courts.

Use leniency. A less drastic alternative is for the lower court fully to utilize whatever discretion it has on sentencing. A light sentence or no sentence may adequately register the trial judge's disapproval of the precedent. But discretion may be limited, and there are no sentences in civil cases.

Recuse or resign. If a particular case raising a particular issue is especially sensitive to a lower court, he can always recuse himself from that one case and avoid the problem. But ultimately the lower-court judge who cannot enforce disagreeable higher court precedents may have to consider resigning from the bench. Being a lower-court judge may entail certain responsibilities so repugnant as to be incapable of performance without injuring or destroying the judge's personality structure.

The range of alternatives is neither wide nor altogether happy. Yet the problem must be a recurring one. And it cuts across politics: For every judge who disagrees with capital punishment, there is a judge opposed to Supreme Court precedents regarding desegregation and procedural safeguards for criminal defendants. What kind of legal system will we have if every lower-court judge can decide for himself which Supreme Court precedents he will adhere to? Is it any different from Southern resistance to the 1954 *Brown* decision? It simply cannot depend on the particular issue.

Perhaps in the end the problem comes down to what we mean by the Constitution. Every federal judge takes an oath to uphold and defend the Constitution. Does that oath refer to the text of the Constitution or the Supreme Court's interpretations of the text?

In 1970, Chief Justice Warren Burger "categorically" rejected the "thesis that what the Court said lately controls over the Constitution." And in 1939, Justice Felix Frankfurter pointed out that "the ultimate touchstone of constitutionality is the Constitution itself and not what we have said about it."

If a judge is sworn to uphold the Constitution, would he be breaking that oath if he followed what he viewed as unacceptable "gloss" put on the Constitution by the Supreme Court? On the other hand, if every official, federal or state or local, who takes an oath to support the Constitution is free to disregard pronouncements of the Supreme Court, the results will be frightening.

The problem is put into stark relief by the dissent in *Hutto* v. *Davis*. Although the majority said that what the Fourth Circuit did was tantamount to "anarchy," the dissent thought the Court of Appeals "has only fulfilled its constitutional responsibility to apply the [Supreme] Court's precedents in light of reason and experience—something that this Court today has plainly failed to do."

30

Boxing and the Legal Process

BOXING has caught the public imagination as perhaps never before. Millions of people pay millions of dollars to watch the good fights. Front-page headlines scream about a $21.3 million bank scandal allegedly involving a boxing promoter. Feature movies about boxing—the *Rocky* series and *Raging Bull*—were popular and artistic successes.

The current public interest should focus attention on the legal aspects of professional boxing. A federal court jury in Manhattan recently rejected an antitrust claim that might have restructured professional boxing. Congress could, if it wanted to, regulate boxing as an aspect of interstate commerce. But up to now, at least, it has chosen not to, and has left the regulation of boxing entirely up to the individual states. State legislatures have passed statutes and created administrative agencies (i.e., athletic or boxing commissions) to govern boxing by issuing regulations and implementing them.

Within the framework of public control represented by state regulation, professional boxing is based primarily on a system of private ordering. Boxers, managers, and promoters have voluntarily formed two rival organizations—the World Boxing Association and the World Boxing Council—that have their own rules as well as separate champions in weight classes. To the extent unregulated by state law, legal relations between boxers, managers, and promoters are a matter of contract law.

At the heart of boxing is the relationship between a boxer and his manager. A boxer gets a manager long before the fighter becomes a contender. Training in a gym, a young, inexperienced, naive, trusting fighter is likely to be approached by an onlooker seeking to manage him. Unrepresented by counsel and often the product of ghetto life, the young boxer is easy prey for a fast-talking potential manager. These realities of the relationship between boxer and manager are the basis for much of the regulation of boxer-manager contracts.

In regulating the relationship between boxers and managers, government has channeled the process of individual bargaining. By means of direct public ordering, law regulates the substantive terms of boxer-manager contracts. It has tried to protect boxers from their own improvident acts as well as from the predatory acts of unscrupulous managers.

Most, if not all, states now have form contracts for boxers and managers to sign. All the parties do is insert their names and the date, a percentage division of future purses, and a term. But there is no real negotiation over even those aspects, for parties routinely provide the maximum percentage for the manager and the maximum length for the contract. Contracts between boxers and managers thus fall into that class of modern contracts involving standardized terms requiring no negotiation.

Contracts without negotiation as to terms are a relatively new development. During much of the past, a contract entailed bargaining between the parties as to each of the terms. The economic forces of the market and the relative economic strength of the two bargainers determined the outcome. It was in that economic setting that classic principles of contract law grew. But as the economic reality changes, and the nature of contract itself is transformed, the principles of contract law need to be reexamined.

The typical boxer's lament is that it is he—not the manager or other members of the entourage—who trains, walks into the ring, and takes the punishment and the risks, and that somehow other people profit at his expense. Part of the problem is due to the way the contract phrases the relative obligations of boxer and manager. Typically, the boxer agrees "to render boxing services, including training, sparring, and boxing in exhibitions and contests at such times and places as designated by the manager," and not to participate in any exhibitions, contests, or training exercises "except as specifically approved or required by the manager." The boxer's services are designated "extraordinary and unique," legal code words that spell relief I-N-J-U-N-C-T-I-O-N. In return for the boxer's efforts, the manager usually gets a third of any purse. Is it any wonder that boxers sometimes feel they work for their managers, and not the other way around?

In sharp contrast, a manager's obligations are phrased less clearly. A manager is usually obligated "to use his best efforts to provide adequate training for the boxer, and to secure for the boxer reasonably remunerative boxing contests and exhibitions against fighters of similar qualifications for skill." But what are "best efforts"? Judicial definitions of "best efforts" abound, yet no definition can infuse such a vague and indefinite phrase with clarity and precision. The result is that it is hard to show that a manager has failed to live up to his contractual commitment.

A manager plays a crucial role in a boxer's career. A good manager must have a variety of skills. He must be able to relate well to his boxer, to win the boxer's trust, to serve as a link between the boxer and the rest of the world, to provide proper training, and, hardest of all to define, inspiration. A manager must choose his boxer's opponents with care, timing, and a sense of how best to advance his boxer through the ranks. He negotiates contracts and often handles the boxer's financial affairs. All in all, a manager can make the difference in a boxer's career.

If a manager's obligations are difficult to verbalize with precision, they might better be viewed as part of a special relationship of trust, a fiduciary relationship. Normally, a manager is far older, more educated, more articulate, and more familiar with the worlds of business and boxing than his boxer. These are some of the reasons why the boxer picks him as his manager. In fact, the identity of parties—which boxer signs on with which manager—is the sole area of choice open to the parties. Each chooses the other based on an assessment of his ability to box or manage. In these circumstances, it would cause no upheaval to treat the boxer-manager relationship as a special trust relationship, a fiduciary relationship, imposing higher standards of loyalty, honor, and duty on the manager in his conduct on behalf of his boxer.

One of the most important aspects of a boxer-manager contract is how long it will be in effect. Experience has shown that managers tend to want longer contracts. A longer contract permits managers to receive more of the benefits of a fighter's good years after advancing him through the ranks. From a manager's point of view, he has most likely advanced funds as well as spent time and effort for the boxer during the lean years with an eye toward reaping a third of larger future purses. The longer the contract, the more purses in which the manager will share.

But inordinately long contracts can work to a fighter's disadvantage. A fighter may outgrow a manager with whom he signed at an early stage of his career. A long contract may make a fighter feel as if he were an indentured servant. And if a dispute arises between boxer and manager, the boxer will feel as if he is working to support someone who is no longer advancing the fighter's career. From the boxer's vantage point, the shorter the contract, the more freedom the fighter has in choosing who will manage him.

Balancing the manager's interest in his investment of time, money, and effort against the boxer's interest in controlling his own career has led government to restrict the term of management contracts. And the trend has been to make the term of such contracts shorter and shorter. As a result of a recent interstate compact, it is now the policy of the New York Athletic Commission not to approve contracts for a term in excess of three years. New Jersey has a two-year limitation.

Despite official policy, managers have been known to try to find ways of extending their contracts beyond the maximum term. Shortly after signing one contract, a boxer and manager may sign another agreement extending the manager's term for an additional term. The net effect of the two management contracts signed within months of each other would purportedly be to have the manager manage the fighter beyond the maximum legal term.

The second contract is known in the business as a "piggyback" contract. It tries to accomplish by indirection what cannot be accomplished directly. The New Jersey State Athletic Commission has ruled that such piggyback contracts are "unconscionable" and would not be recognized in that state.

To avoid problems over the term of a management contract, some consideration ought to be given to including in the form contract a termination clause. Such a clause could, as it does in ordinary employment agreements, spell out exactly how the parties could terminate the agreement before it expires. Even if the sole ground for termination is "cause," the agreement could define "cause" and specify what procedure should be followed if one of the parties wishes to terminate for "cause." One of the problems in this regard is the amorphous nature of the services rendered, especially the manager's duty to use his "best efforts" to advance the fighter's career. Inclusion of some type of a termination clause would therefore be in the interest of both parties.

Boxers and managers form only two of three sides of the boxing triangle. The third side consists of promoters. Promoters arrange boxing shows. A promoter's role is to sign a contract with a particular boxer or boxers for a fight on a given date for an agreed on consideration to be paid by the promoter to the boxer after the fight. The promoter then enters into a contract with network television or closed-circuit television or radio for broadcasting the fight. The promoter may receive a proportional part of the live-gate receipts from the site owner and earns income from the sale of any other ancillary contracts, including broadcast or telecast rights. The promoter's profit is the difference between the promoter's income from all sources less his expenses in promoting the fight.

Promotion contracts are also subject to public ordering. Many of the regulations governing managers have analogues for promoters, and for many of the same reasons. Promoters, like managers, have to be licensed. Their contracts, both standardized form contracts issued by the states and privately negotiated agreements, still must be publicly disclosed. A promoter cannot act as a manager, and vice versa. Sometimes, although the problems may be similar, the solutions are different. The duration of a promoter's contract is a case in point.

Promoters prefer to be able to sign a fighter to a contract giving the promoter an option to promote the boxer's future fights. So-called option contracts typically offer a fighter a considerably higher purse than a one-fight contract, but at the price of the fighter's freedom to negotiate with other promoters for higher purses in the future. From a promoter's angle of vision, such an arrangement may be justified economically. A promoter will pay a fighter in excess of his drawing capacity in one fight and lose money on a fighter unless there was some assurance that the fighter would be available to be promoted again.

But option contracts may represent too great a sacrifice of the fighter's freedom. Although the states have not regulated in this area, New Jersey Deputy Commissioner Robert Lee has called such contracts a form of "involuntary servitude." The problem is that the fighter may sign an option contract because of an irresistible purse but as a result may significantly limit his future purses. To prevent this problem, WBA Regulation 7 prohibits promoters from signing fighters to option contracts. But despite WBA Regulation 7, option contracts are quite common, even from the most reputable promoters. Apparently, option contracts will not end until either the states adopt WBA Regulation 7 as law or the courts start refusing to enforce option contracts.

In a business where the boxer has often had the least to say, this new concern for the boxer's interest is welcome. In one recent case, Don King Productions, Inc. sought a preliminary injunction to stop Bob Arum's Top Rank, Inc. from promoting a light heavyweight bout involving a boxer with whom King claimed to have an option contract. Without deciding whether or not the option was enforceable, but expressing doubts on that score, the court refused to grant the injunction because the boxer himself was not a party to the action.

Although aware that the rival promoters had "a large financial stake in the outcome," the court pointed out that "the boxer in question is an athlete with an opportunity to gain a world championship. He has a large financial and career stake in whether or not the bout goes on. Although [the boxer] is the subject of this action, he is not an article of personal property subject to an attachment proceeding, but a human being who risks his health and perhaps his life in what must of physical necessity be a limited number of engagements."

Such a judicial attitude, if it takes hold, may signal important shifts in how professional boxing operates.

The hybrid system of public control and private ordering that governs boxing today is in jeopardy. Professional boxing may become the main event in a new effort to struggle with the problem of allocating power in a free society between public and private systems of government. We may all have ringside seats to a new allocation among various institutions of government of the responsibility of formulating the public policies and legal rules for boxing, including the primordial public policy of the extent to which governmental control shall supplant or channel private ordering.

31

Inherited Wealth and
the Constitution

Now is a good time to consider the relationship between inherited wealth and democratic thinking. Congress recently debated how much to relax estate and gift taxes. It assumed that such taxes should be eased, and even spurred speculation that total repeal may not be far off. Inasmuch as estate and gift taxes have never been large revenue raisers, tinkering with them may indicate a shift in our view of the underlying purposes of such taxes.

Estate taxes are our society's reasonable compromise to reduce the tension between two basic values. One value, liberty, suggests that an individual has the right to do whatever he wants with his property. On the other hand, a free society has a strong commitment to the value of equality of opportunity. Balancing these values is the task of the current congressional debate, which is the latest round in an old controversy over a hard problem for American political theory.

I

Past debates about inheritance of wealth have weighed it in social terms, supported or condemned it for its good or bad effects on society, for its fairness, justness, or morality.

For the most part, no arguments have been made based on the United States Constitution. But the Constitution may have something to say on the subject, something unnoticed all these years, yet something that should be a part of any current debate.

It may be that a constitutional argument (not based on a contrived violation of "equal protection of the laws") can be made *against* inheritance of wealth.

This constitutional argument hinges on rather obscure provisions that could truly turn out to be sleeping giants. Not once but twice the Constitution prohibits "Titles of Nobility." Section 9 of Article I restricts the federal government and declares: "No Title of Nobility shall be granted by the United States." And Section 10 of Article I provides: "No state shall . . . grant any Title of Nobility." The crucial question is whether inheritance of wealth is in tension with the values represented by the constitutional ban on titles of nobility.

Such a ban goes back to the year of our independence. A prohibition against titles of nobility first appeared in a 1776 draft of the Articles of Confederation. It existed in the final draft, and was adopted by the Constitutional Convention in 1787.

The available evidence is scant but clearly shows that the Framers meant the Titles of Nobility Clauses to embody a fundamental break with European aristocracies. The clauses were viewed as absolutely essential to the American revolt against rank and birth typical of the Old World.

In No. 84 of *The Federalist*, Hamilton stressed the role of the Titles of Nobility Clauses as "securities to liberty and republicanism." Later in the same number, Hamilton goes on: "Nothing need be said to illustrate the importance of the prohibition of titles of nobility. This may truly be denominated the cornerstone of republican government; for so long as they are excluded there can never be serious danger that the government will be any other than that of the people."

In Federalist No. 39, Madison, criticizing governments of "hereditary aristocracy and monarchy," wrote: "Could any further proof be required of the republican complexion of this system [i.e., the system under the proposed federal constitution], the most decisive one might be found in its absolute prohibition of titles of nobility, both under the federal and state governments."

Joseph Story, in his *Commentaries on the Constitution*, also called the Titles of Nobility Clauses "a cornerstone of republican government," and explained: "As a perfect equality in the basis of all of our institutions, state and national, the prohibition against the creation of any titles of nobility seems proper, if not indispensable, to keep perpetually alive a just sense of this important truth. Distinctions between citizens in regard to rank would soon lay the foundations of odious claims and privileges, and silently subvert the spirit of independence and personal dignity, which are so often proclaimed to be the best security of a republican government."

The Titles of Nobility Clauses reflected the Founders' hatred of artificial aristocracy. Jefferson, in a letter to John Adams, said, "There is a natural aristocracy among men. The grounds of this are virtue and talents." To which Jefferson contrasted "an artificial aristocracy, founded on wealth and birth, without either virtue or talents." A natural aristocracy, Jefferson believed, was "the most precious gift of nature."

"Of wealth," Jefferson continued, "there were great accumulations in particular families, handed down from generation to generation, under the English law of entails . . . At the first session of our legislature after the Declaration of Independence, we passed a law abolishing entails. And this was followed by one abolishing the privilege of primogeniture. These laws, drawn by myself, laid the axe to the foot of pseudo-aristocracy."

Beaumarchais, the Frenchman most responsible for French logistical support of the American Revolution, incorporated our revolutionary ideals in his literary work. In the early 1780s, he wrote "The Marriage of Figaro," a controversially popular play that contained the stirring lines spoken by Figaro to the Spanish grandees, "What have you done to earn so many advantages? You took the trouble to be born, nothing more. Apart from that, you're rather a common type." This famous passage by Beaumarchais has earned a reputation as the "harbinger of revolution."

Such attitudes tend toward the conclusion that the Titles of Nobility Clauses must have been conceived as more than literal, narrow proscriptions against calling someone a duke or an earl. The evil they were designed to correct was an artificially stratified society. They were born in the Enlightenment with a bold, broad purpose.

The Titles of Nobility Clauses should be interpreted as part of a living document. Just as concepts of "cruel and unusual punishment" and "equal protection of the laws," for example, have evolved over time, so too has the concept of "title of nobility." Inheritance of wealth can readily be seen as the modern-day equivalent of a "title of nobility." We can functionally define "title of nobility" as a heritable privilege granted by the State without regard to performance or individual achievement. Such a definition encompasses inheritance of wealth.

This new constitutional argument will startle and unsettle many people. Prevailing views about inheritance are too well established to suffer a turnabout overnight. But it is not unreasonable to hope that the Titles of Nobility Clauses will add a new constitutional perspective to debates about inheritance. Debates about inheritance—including legislative debates—should henceforth have constitutional overtones previously ignored, at least if the debates are to be faithful to important values in the Constitution.

II

Merely to entertain doubts about the constitutionality of inherited wealth is terribly distressing. A practice so old and widespread is bound to have staunch defenders. But any defense of inherited wealth should be grounded on more than sheer economic self-interest. It should have a theoretical basis. Thinking through the implications of the argument based on the Titles of Nobility Clauses permits us to look more carefully at the underpinnings of the institution of inherited wealth and at least to note, if not answer, the large questions inevitably raised.

The most common criticism of any plan to abolish inheritance is that abolition amounts to socialism, manic egalitarianism, and even communism. But abolishing inheritance may really be a truer form of meritocracy, competition, and individualism. Although abolition would mean each generation would start out equal in terms of wealth, *within each generation* inequalities would arise proportional to the money-making abilities of each individual. The inequalities that would inevitably develop are the very opposite of socialism, egalitarianism, and communism.

When critics of abolishing inheritance invoke the buzz word socialism, they probably reflect the belief that a person should have the right to leave his wealth to whomever he wants—the right of freedom of testation. They would claim that freedom of testation is a natural right protected by the Constitution as part of the liberty included within substantive due process. In this camp can be found some of the most ardent conservative thinkers—Ayn Rand, Robert Nozick, and F. A. Hayek, for example—who, curiously, fail to see the contradictions between their support of meritocracy, individualism, and free competition, on the one hand, and their support of inherited wealth, on the other.

Apart from this basic contradiction, the notion of a natural right of freedom of testation is belied by the long history of estate taxes and by the holdings of a vast array of American courts, including the Supreme Court, that freedom of testation is a purely statutory right and can be wholly taken away by the legislature. As the Supreme Court said over a hundred years ago, "The right to take property by devise or descent is the creature of law and not a natural right."

It is unfair and inaccurate to say that abolishing inheritance is simply a way of confiscating the property of the people once every generation. Death is, so to speak, a natural cutoff. Once a person dies, he no longer exists and it is a bootstrapping legal fiction to argue that any property that belonged to him in life is "confiscated" at death. Death breaks the chain of legal relationships between the owner and his property.

Property, of course, is not the only advantage that is inherited. Talent, ability, beauty, and intelligence are all to some extent inherited and unearned. Is Jefferson right in distinguishing wealth from other inherited advantages (biological and environmental) on the ground that inherited wealth creates an artificial aristocracy and conflicts with notions of a natural aristocracy, a "career open to talent," and "meritocracy"? Or is it morally wrong and socially unjust, as Harvard philosopher John Rawls *(A Theory of Justice)* believes, to reward people on the basis of traits they have not earned or deserved?

It is often said that inheritance is an incentive for accumulating wealth and therefore an incentive for the utmost in productive effort during life. No one has researched, statistically or otherwise, that statement. It is speculative. On its face, it looks like the product of cultural conditioning.

Doing away with inherited wealth, according to Andrew Carnegie in his 1889 article "The Gospel of Wealth," would not "sap the root of enterprise and render men less anxious to accumulate, for, to the class whose ambition it is to leave great fortunes and be talked about after their death, it will attract even more attention, and, indeed, be a somewhat nobler ambition, to have enormous sums paid over to the State from their fortunes."

The debate over inherited wealth may refine the American Dream. The American Dream has always meant the hope of a better life, for one's self and one's children as well. But a question arises whether the Dream meant for children to benefit from their parents' wealth or from the opportunities in America for their own success. This difference is crucial for the issue of inherited wealth.

If all intergenerational transmission of wealth is outlawed, would it be necessary to plug the loopholes to *inter vivos* gifts and trusts? Would we want, by law, to prevent a King Lear syndrome whereby parents would during their lives give away their wealth to their children and live to see their children spurn and scorn them?

Does the type of wealth make a difference? For instance, would it be proper to distinguish farmland worked by one family for generations from liquid assets? During the recent debate, several congressmen said that small farms, due to estate taxes, have been bought up by the large corporate agricultural businesses. This new development adds an element of industrial organization to the debate.

Carnegie, a true Horatio Alger hero, left no doubts on

which side of the debate he stood. "The growing disposition to tax more and more heavily large estates left at death," he wrote, "is cheering indication of the growth of a salutary change in public opinion." Distinguishing a person's right to accumulate a fortune during life, Carnegie wrote that, "It is difficult to set bounds to the share of a rich man's estate which should go at his death to the public through the agency of the State."

In a larger sense, abolition of inherited wealth may fit into an historical movement identified by Sir Henry Maine in his *Ancient Law*. "The movement of the progressive societies," wrote Maine in 1864, "has hitherto been a movement from Status to Contract." In this statement, Maine refers to the process by which, "The Individual is substituted for the family, as the unit of which civil laws take account." Inherited wealth is one of the symbols of Status, one of "the powers and privileges anciently residing in the Family." Under this interpretation of Maine's theory, abolition of inherited wealth reduces the importance of family status, focuses attention on the individual, and thereby represents the Idea of Progress.

The few issues touched on here are by no means all of the issues implicated by a debate over estate-tax reform. But even these few issues show quite clearly that the institution of inheritance of wealth involves basic value choices related to some of the most fundamental aspects of our society. Noted tax authority Boris Bittker has observed, "The history of the relationship of democratic thinking to the institution of inheritance is still to be written." Even if not yet written, that history should be part of any debate over estate tax reform.

32

Marriage as a Business Enterprise

As NEW YORK courts start to interpret the new equitable distribution law in divorce cases, we may learn that we are viewing marriage in the wrong light. There may be nothing wrong with the institution of marriage; the trouble is our approach to it.

The trick is to look at marriage from another perspective. People often say marriage is like a joint venture or a partnership, and some modern couples even have marriage contracts. Thinking of marriage metaphorically as a business enterprise, while perhaps not entirely satisfying emotionally, is suggestive. The suggestion brought to mind is the business world, the world of corporations.

Suppose that marriages were treated as corporations. Think of all the advantages.

To start with, a couple that wanted to form a marital corporation no longer would need to apply for a marriage license. They would simply file a certificate of incorporation.

To manage the marital corporation, the incorporators would write by-laws (not to be confused with in-laws), which would operate much as soon-to-be outmoded marriage contracts. The two incorporators would serve as officers, directors, and stockholders. Depending on the wishes of the incorporators, other persons—such as parents, brothers, or sisters—might be designated as directors, and additional stock may be issued to various interested persons.

Marriage manuals would disappear from the shelves. They would be replaced by books on managing corporations. Newly formed marital corporations, rather than spend a passionate week in a hotel room with a heart-shaped bathtub, will replace the outmoded honeymoon with a week on the floor of the New York Stock Exchange.

Children could be treated as wholly owned subsidiaries, and when they move away from the home office, as spin-offs.

When the marital corporation needs money, it would not have to face the often trying task of obtaining personal loans at high interest rates. As a corporation, it could raise from the sale of various corporate securities. Common stock, preferred stock, bonds, convertibles, warrants, and options would all then be available for the purpose.

Financial trouble for the marital corporation need not lead to the breakdown of the marriage. Reorganization, bankruptcy, and general assignment would become reasonable ways to cope.

Depreciation policies, mergers, tender offers, public trading of securities, and regulation by the Securities and Exchange Commission all raise possibilities that tickle the imagination.

Separation might be treated as a form of reorganization. Marriage counselors would be replaced by conventional equity receivers. Alimony and child support would soon be no more than corporate liquidations to stockholders. Adoption would call for nothing more than a simple acquisition agreement.

Divorce, that ugly word, would be forever banished. We would never again hear of the skyrocketing divorce rate. Instead, we would have just another form of voluntary corporate dissolution, accomplished by filing the appropriate piece of paper with the proper governmental authority.

Where would all this lead? At least not to divorce court.